Sociology of Literature

Sociology of Literature

Subhash Sharma

RAWAT PUBLICATIONS
Jaipur • New Delhi • Bangalore • Hyderabad • Guwahati • Kolkata

ISBN 978-81-316-0613-1

Published by
Prem Rawat for **Rawat Publications**
Satyam Apts, Sector 3, Jawahar Nagar, Jaipur 302 004 (India)
Phone: 0141 265 1748 / 7006 Fax: 0141 265 1748
E-mail: info@rawatbooks.com
Website: www.rawatbooks.com

New Delhi Office
4858/24, Ansari Road, Daryaganj, New Delhi 110 002
Phone: 011 2326 3290

Also at *Bangalore, Hyderabad, Guwahati* and *Kolkata*

Typeset by Rawat Computers, Jaipur
Printed at Chaman Enterprises, New Delhi

Dedicated to
Professor Yogendra Singh
from whom I learnt the most

Contents

Acknowledgement

Writing a book is an individual creation but requires views and comments of others in order to fine-tune the draft. One always learns, unlearns and re-learns from teachers, students, colleagues, friends and readers in more than one way. And, I am not an exception. It is my privilege and pleasure to have a creative and critical interaction on different occasions with Prof Yogendra Singh, Prof K.L. Sharma, Prof Hetukar Jha, Prof Avijit Pathak, Prof Anand Kumar, Mr Sanjay Kumar, Dr Khagendra Thakur, Prof Arun Kamal, Mr Anant Kumar Singh and Mr Jawahar Panday, to cut the long list short. I sincerely thank them from the core of my heart. I also acknowledge the contribution of my family members, especially my wife and children, in preparing this book in more than one way. However, for any error or gap, I am solely responsible.

Subhash Sharma

Preface

The universe of the present study is that of Hindi novels. The novel is a new literary genre of modern age concerned with the contemporary culture, politics, economy and society as a whole whereas, other genres of literature are unable to express social life of human beings in totality. It 'discovers' (and only it can discover) new facts, events, processes, institutions or structures, which were either absolutely unknown or only partly known or known in a disguised/different form to the outside world, That is why it is called 'prose epics' of modern age. Further, as Kundera rightly observes, the novel's spirit is the 'spirit of complexity', that is, as life is complex and complicated, so is the novel. The study of Hindi novels can bring to light, it is hoped, the vision and aspiration of the Hindi-speaking belt which is very large in the country. The present author has remained in close touch with the literary world of Hindi and also has been using it as his mother tongue. This fact helps in understanding and exploring nuances of Hindi literature in general and Hindi novels in particular. It is the official language of Union of India, spoken by almost half of India's population in the entire Hindi belt consisting of UP, Bihar, Rajasthan, MP, Jharkhand, Chhattisgarh, Uttarakhand, Haryana, Himachal Pradesh and Delhi. While it is the first language in Hindi states, it is the second language in many other states. Further, it is also spoken in dozens of other countries. Thus, Hindi novels cover a wider area of writing as well as readership.

Here, we take up various issues of sociology of literature theory and content analysis of selected Hindi novels by (a) identifying the socio-cultural base, (b) analysis of dalit and non-dalit interactions, (c) explaining in socio-cultural terms whether dalits protest or not, (d) analysis of novelist's background and vision; which sort of realism works in the novels? (e) analysis of the message conveyed by each novel, (f) time and place, (g) characters, (h) events, and (i) inter-connections.

The number of Hindi novels published in India every year is quite large. Due to constraints of time, only four Hindi novels have been selected here for sociological analysis. Of these four Hindi novels, two were written before India's independence (1947) and the other two in post-independence period. Independence of India was a major national event; it certainly had its due impact on literary writings. During the British period, freedom struggle was a national phenomenon which either directly or indirectly affected literary writings. After independence, a new era of democracy began here whose influence on literary writings cannot be ruled out. Hence, a comparative study of novels of these two periods may be more useful. These four novels are *Rangbhumi* by Premchand, *Budhua ki Beti* by Pandey Bechan Sharma 'Ugra', *Dharti Dhan Na Apna* by Jagdish Chandra and *Parishishta* by Giriraj Kishor. While *Dharti Dhan Na Apna* is based in the undivided Punjab (of 1950s), the rest three novels are based in Uttar Pradesh.

These novels have dalits as central characters. All the four novelists have been famous in varying degrees. However, Premchand is the most famous writer, called 'Upanyas Samrat' (the emperor of novels). 'Ugra' has also been famous but more controversial due to his provocative writings, different from the prevailing conventional streams. Giriraj Kishor and Jagdish Chandra are relatively less famous but their novels have been noteworthy from the viewpoint of readers as well as critics. The content analysis of these novels would be used with a sociological perspective of studying social relationships between dalits and non-dalits in the larger social system. It is hoped that students of Hindi literature and sociology will benefit in some way or other from this book.

1

Introduction

Sociology of literature developed in Europe in the nineteenth century. In the beginning, it was considered to be a branch of sociology of knowledge, which chiefly dealt with the relationship between knowledge and existence. Sociology of knowledge has remained concerned with the problem of social conditioning of knowledge. Karl Mannheim argued in this context that "mental structures are inevitably differently formed in different social and historical settings".[1] He distinguished the sociology of knowledge from ideology which means 'specific assertions' regarded as concealments, falsifications or lies without incorporating the 'total mental structure' of the asserting subject whereas the sociology of knowledge deals with this very mental structure 'in its totality'. That is, sociology of knowledge does not critically analyse thought on the level of assertions themselves (involving the deceptions and disguises), rather examines it on the structural level. Therefore, he uses the term 'perspective' (not ideology) to refer to "the subject's whole mode of conceiving things as determined by his historical and social settings".[2] This perspective has three elements:

(a) The way one views an object;
(b) What one perceives in it; and
(c) How one construes it in one's thinking.

He also talks of transmission of knowledge from one generation to another, and this relationship between different generations is one of the bases of collective existence and historical experience. He traces the origin of a thought model in the social position of a group and its mode of interpreting the world. By social groups, he means not only the classes, but also generations, status groups, sects, occupational groups, schools, etc.[3]

However, Mannheim admits that class stratification is the most important because "in the final analysis, all the other social groups arise from and are transformed as part of the more basic conditions of production and domination".[4] Further, Mannheim is of the view that "the conditions of existence affect not merely the historical genesis of ideas but constitute the essential part of the products of thought and make themselves felt in their content and form".[5] Before Mannheim, there were three major streams of development in sociology of knowledge:[6]

(a) The German philosophical-sociological tradition reflected in the works of nineteenth century folk psychologists;
(b) French sociology pioneered by Durkheim as well as French crowd psychologists; and
(c) Chicago school of sociology and American social behaviourists (John Dewey, C.H. Cooley and G.H. Mead).

Madame de Stael was the first scholar to use sociological concepts in order to understand the origin of the characteristics of ancient and modern literatures. She was of the view that German literature was the only literature that had begun with criticism. Later Taine, a French sociologist, developed a full-fledged positivistic theory of sociology of literature in order to study it objectively. However, it was Ian Watt who, for the first time, made a thorough sociological study of novels in his book *The Rise of the Novel* (1957) wherein he pointed out that three English novelists, Defoe, Richardson and Fielding are of the same generation and took a realistic view in their novels because of specific favourable literary and social conditions. Watt pointed out a very important aspect of the sociology of knowledge that "the novel's realism does not reside in the kind of life it presents but in the way it presents it".[7] Thus, with this sociological perspective, he compared the eighteenth century novels of English and French philosophical realism. He traced that there was a linkage between increase in the number of novels and increase in the size of the reading public due to rise in education, development of libraries, suppression of patronage by the booksellers, and the fall in the price of books in general and of novels in particular. Similarly, Bakhtin synthesised formalism and Marxism for the study of literature. Georg Lukacs emphasised on the community in the novel on the one hand (as in epics) and, on the other hand, argued that a novel should take into account the radical opposition between man and the world. Further, Goldmann and Lowenthal also developed the sociology of literature in their own ways. Goldman through his 'genetic structuralism', argues Leenhardt, focuses on an understanding of the meaning of work, i.e., "clarifying the total network of meanings which internal analysis of a work reveals by an explanation by the insertion of this network in a whole of wider significance: the social group".[8]

Milan Kundera rightly points out that Cervantes was a great novelist and his novel *Don Quixot* set off into a world gradually that opened wide before him and "a great European art took shape that is nothing other than the investigation of this forgotten being".[9] He is of the view that "the founder of the Modern Era is not only Descartes but also Cervantes".[10] According to Kundera, novel is a European creation of modern age but it came to a halt during Russian communism and the novel died there because "totalitarian truth excludes relativity, doubt, questions; it can never accommodate what I would call the spirit of the novel".[11] Thus, it is clear that for the emergence and growth of novel as a form of literature, various social conditions such as the rise of new middle class, increase in education, leisure, printing technology, market, freedom of expression, etc., seem to be necessary. He also explains that a novelist actually writes a kind of 'theme' in the first novel and other novels are 'variations'.[12] This is true about himself. He further points out that there are three possibilities for the novelist: (a) he *tells* a story (e.g., Fielding); (b) he *describes* a story (e.g., Flaubert); and (c) he *thinks* a story (e.g., Musil). The nineteenth century novel of 'description' was in coherence with the positivistic spirit of the time.[13] Kundera contends that there is not a single history of the novel, rather there are histories of the novel – the Chinese novel, Greco-Roman, Japanese, Medieval, etc.[14] He also defines novel "as the great prose form in which an author thoroughly exposes by means of experiment of selves (characters), some great things of existence".[15] Ralph Fox is not far from this view and considers novel as "the epic art form of our modern, bourgeois society"[16] depicting ordinary events of daily life. A novel has many elements such as plot, character, dialogue, time and place, style, and world vision.[17] Forster mentions different aspects of novel: story, people, plot, fantasy, prophecy, pattern and rhythm.[18]

The Rise of Hindi Novels (1870–1890)

According to one opinion, the first Hindi novel was *Devrani Jethani Ki Kahani,* written by Gauri Dutt.[19] It was the first original fiction about a new subject from ordinary world published from Meerut (UP) in 1870. There is another view that holds *Bhagyawati* as the first novel in Hindi. It was written by Shraddharam Phillauri in 1877, but was published, according to Vijay Shankar Malla, in 1887.[20] Its fifth edition came out by 1912 and was prescribed as a text book for the education of girls in government schools.[21] However, many scholars do not accept *Bhagyawati* as the first Hindi novel because it was not an original literary creation. There is a third opinion according to which *Pariksha Guru* (1882) was the first Hindi novel, as asserted by noted Hindi critic Ram Chandra Shukla.[22] This novel was written by Lala Shriniwas Das, and published by Sadadarsh Press, Delhi. Some scholars like Kunwar Pal Singh[23] praise the utilitarian perspective and morality of the rising middle class in the novel *Pariksha Guru*. However, during the nineteenth century, many other novels were also published. For example, *Rahasya Katha Upanyas* was written by the noted writer Balkrishna Bhatt (1879) but it was incomplete.

Similarly, Bhartendu Harishchandra wrote an incomplete novel *Ek Kahani Kuchh Ap Biti, Kuchh Jag Biti* (1879). Further *Gupta Bairi*, another incomplete novel, was written by Balkrishna Bhatt and published in 1882. His other novel was *Nutan Brahmachari* (1886). In 1881, Radha Krishna Das wrote *Nissahay Hindu* but it was published in 1890. It was about Hindu-Muslim harmony.

Hindi novels, written between 1870 and 1890 were more imaginary and less realistic since there was a movement for renaissance in the Hindi belt only after its inception in Bengal and Maharashtra. Actually, Hindi renaissance began with the revolt of 1857, which was the first freedom movement of India. However, it was a new kind of enlightenment from a political perspective only and in the social arena, renaissance began with the formation of Arya Samaj in 1875.[24] Therefore, many Hindi writers of that period were influenced by the reforms of the Arya Samaj movement and they passionately highlighted the positive aspects of Indian culture and the negative aspects of Western culture. Secondly, there was a didactic tendency among the novelists to reform what they considered superstitions, rituals and bad customs. For example, the novels of Kishorilal Goswami, Lajja Ram Mehta, Balkrishna Bhatt, etc., contained such tendencies. Besides Arya Samaj, there were also some estates in north India that promoted the cause of Hindi novels. For instance, the then ruler of Darbhanga estate, Lakshmishwar Singh declared an award of 150 rupees in August 1880 for writing 'Gadya Kavya Upanyas' (novel) and this award was given to Devakinandan Tripathi of Prayag for his novel *Amrit Charitra* in 1881.[25]

Thus, during the period between 1870 and 1890, Hindi novels had very much linkage with the then prevailing trends of renaissance. The major features of such novels were as follows:[26]

(a) In the rise of European novels, capitalist economy and middle class played a major role, whereas during 1870–1890 there was neither a capitalist economy nor a strong middle class in Hindi society in India.

(b) In the novels written during 1870–1890, generally the life and society of upper middle class was depicted. Hindi novels did not emerge due to the demand of the middle class, rather it developed in course of Hindi writers' attempt for highlighting their sense of nationalism. After the failure of 1857 revolt, a sense of pan-Indian nationalism had begun to develop. Consequently, women's education, widow remarriage, child marriage, conspicuous expenditure in marriage, etc., became issues of concern for intellectuals and writers.

(c) Some novelists of this period raised the issue of progress of Hindi language. A conflict of supporting and opposing English education is depicted in the novels of this period. Most of the novels opposed the copying of Western manners, eating habits and lifestyles, though they supported Western science and technology, trade and commerce.

(d) In most of the novels of this period there was no inkling of lovemaking before marriage as it was not allowed in the Indian social system at that time.

(e) In this regard, no conflict of moral values can be discerned from these novels as most of the characters were presented as following some known social values. Those characters who were shown violating such values were villains who were punished and reformed.

(f) The structure of most of these novels is simple and one-dimensional, i.e., single story is presented with one dimension of characters. The story-world of such novels is very small (often limited to family) though nature as well as moral teachings are depicted in detail. But, observes Gopal Roy, "due to brevity of activities there is very little complexity in their plots. Consequently there was no scope of experiment in their form too".

(g) The novels of this period have two parallel traditions as far as language is concerned. While Balkrishna Bhatt, Kishorilal Goswami and Jaganmohan Singh used a sophisticated (Sanskritised) literary Hindi as followed in

Sanskrit prose-epics, others like Gauri Dutt, Radhakrishna Das, Lala Srinivas Das, Ishwari Prasad and Kalyan Rai used common Hindi of daily use.

Hindi Novels 1891–1917 (pre-Premchand Era)

The next period of romantic and thriller novels began in 1891 and ended in 1917. The first part of *Chandra Kanta* was written in 1887 by Devki Nandan Khatri and published in 1888–92. *Chandra Kanta* was a very popular creation. Later Khatri wrote *Chandra Kanta Santati* (1894–1905). It also became very popular and several editions of these novels were brought out on public demand. Many non-Hindi knowing people learnt Hindi to read and enjoy these creative works. The major features of the novels of this period (1891–1917)[27] are as follows:

(a) By this period the number of Hindi novel readers increased very much due to crime-related stories, romantic stories, fantasies and detective novels. This large group of readers was mainly from the middle class that became both the subject-matter and purchaser-reader. Secondly, Hindi novels, which developed due to the efforts of Devaki Nandan Khatri, Kishorilal Gowswami, Gopal Ram Gahmari, corresponded to European 'fiction' rather than European novels. Though Bhuvneshwar Mishra, Raj Nandan Sahay, Mehta Lajja Ram Sharma, etc., based their writings on social realism, yet most of the novels oriented towards fiction.

(b) Most of the novels of this period were based on past events in their novels. For instance, Kishorilal Goswami's *Sultana, Razia Begum, Tara,* etc., conveyed a glorified picture of Indian society of ancient period.

(c) Physical love was a popular theme of the novels of this period. For instance, Kishorilal Goswami focused more on physical love at the cost of the deeper sensitivity. However, Bhuvneshwar Mishra emphasised on the sensitivity aspect in his novel *Balwant Bhumihar*, but he was an exception.

(d) In these novels also, there was no conflict of value (except in *Balwant Bhumihar)* – most of the characters followed the ideals established by such novelists.

(e) Most of the novels of the period were concerned with education, progress of Hindi language, European technology while rejecting European way of living, eating habits, etc.

(f) Most of these novels did not directly oppose the British rule though dissatisfaction with the working of police force and government offices is expressed invariably – depiction of functional problems, not structural problems.

(g) Most of the novels of this period had little concern for the rural masses.

(h) A complex plot was constructed in most of the novels. It made them more authentic.

(i) Most of the novelists are present in the novels as 'story-tellers' as if they wanted to help the readers having difficulty to understand the complex situation.

(j) In this period also, there were two parallel styles of writing Hindi: Sanskritised literary Hindi, and dialect of common use. While Kishorilal Goswami, Bhuvneshwar Mishra, Mannan Dwivedi, Mehta Lajja Ram Sharma, Brajnandan Sahai and Gajpuri focused on creative literary language, Devaki Nandan Khatri (who is sometimes disputed to be a novelist) focused on common spoken language.

Novels of 1918–1936 (Premchand Era)

During 1918–1936, contemporary society was in the centre of Hindi novels. Premchand wrote his first novel *Seva Sadan* in 1918 about the problems of prostitutes. Afterwards, he wrote many famous novels such as *Premashram* (1922), *Rangbhumi* (1925), *Kayakalp* (1926), *Nirmala* (1927), *Gaban* (1931), *Karmbhumi* (1932) and *Godan* (1936) in Hindi and a few novels in Urdu. His last novel Mangalsutra remained incomplete. Second important novelist of the period was Pandey Bechan Sharma 'Ugra', who became known for depicting rigorously and courageously the social customs and bad practices like drinking, prostitution and dalit problems. His important novels are *Chand Hasinon Ke Khatut* (1927), *Dilli Ka Dalal* (1928), *Budhua Ki Beti* (1928), *Sharabi* (1930), *Karhi Mein Koyala* (1955), *Sarkar Tumhari Ankhon Mein* (1937), *Jijiji'* (1939) *and Fagun Ke Din Char* (1960). Shiv. Pujan Sahai wrote a novel *Dehati Duniya* in 1926, which is known as the first regional novel in Hindi. Jaishankar Prasad was another important novelist of this period. He wrote three novels *Kankal (*1932), *Titali* (1934) and Irawati (incomplete) in 1936. He depicted exploitation of women and dalits in Kankal and, he depicted the tortures by government machinery in Titali. During that period, Suryakant Tripathi 'Nirala' also wrote four novels – *Apsara* (1931), *Alka* (1933), *Nirupama* (1936) and *Prabhawati* (1936). However, his novels could not succeed as much as his poetry, as he failed to realistically depict the complex society because of his focused poetic vision. Bhagwati Charan Varma was another famous novelist of the period whose novel *Chitralekha* was one of the most popular novels of the period. It is very philosophical about what is sin and what is its status. Siyaram Sharan Gupta wrote an important novel *Nari* wherein the compulsions and helplessness of women is depicted. Ila Chandra Joshi, taking a psychological stand, wrote a novel *Ghrinamayee* wherein the inner life of human beings is depicted. Later Jainendra Kumar depicted the inner life and mental conflict of man. He wrote a popular novel *Sunita* (1935) who loves her paramour without being disloyal to her husband. His other novels are *Tyagapatra* (1937) and *Kalyani.* He questioned the traditional and typified role of women. Vrindavan Lal Varma wrote *Garh Kundhar* and other novels in which he used popular sayings, folktales and archeological evidences for constructing historical narrations.

During Premchand's period, quite a number of women writers wrote about a dozen of novels and depicted the precarious condition of widows, husband-wife conflicts, prostitution, etc. Usha Devi Mitra wrote a novel *Vachan ka Mol* where the problem of love and marriage has been depicted in a very complex manner. There were said to be two schools of novels, one of idealistic realism led by Premchand and other of naturalism led by 'Ugra'. However, to be fair, 'Ugra' and 'Prasad' were pioneers of 'subaltern realism' (to use Gopal Roy's terms) wherein the dalit characters got prominence on the centre stage of Hindi novels.[28]

The minor novels such as Bhagwat Prasad Shukla's *Bharat Premi* (1919), Mohini Mohan's *Deshoddhar* (1920), Krishnalal Varma's *Punaruddhar* (1921), Chhavinath Pandey's *Protsahan* (1921) courageously depicted India's freedom movement whereas famous writers like Premchand were more cautious in this regard. Further, the problems of prostitutes are one of the major subject matters of novels of this period. Most of the novels of this period had common mass language whereas a few others of Jaishanker Prasad and Nirala had Sanskritised literary Hindi.

Novels of 1937–1947 (post-Premchand Era)

During 1937–1947, in post-Premchand period, new waves of thinking became visible. For example, *Tyagpatra* and *Kalyani* novels by Jainendra Kumar reacted sharply at the traditional Hindi social system. Premchand had predicted that Hindi novels in future would be more character-oriented. Jainendra's novels had heroes and their activities for depiction. S.H. Vatsyayan 'Agyeya' wrote *Shekhar: Ek Jivani*, whose first part was published in 1940 and second part was published in 1944. Shekhar, the hero of Agyeye, was a rebel by birth and was deeply concerned with understanding himself. Yashpal wrote *Dada Comrade* in 1941 with a perspective of communist ideology. His other novels are *Divya* (1945), *Deshdrohi* (1943) and *Party Comrade*. The activist-writer Rahul Sankrityayan wrote *Singh Senapati* (1944) and *Jai Yaudheya* (1944). He depicted equality between men and women in Vaishali and Takshashila republics of ancient period. Hajari Prasad Dwivedi wrote *Banabhatt Ki Atmakatha* in 1946 that displays his unique craft of using history for literary creation. Later Brindavanlal Varma wrote *Jhansi Ki Rani Lakshmi Bai* (1946) based on British Indian history wherein a sense of nationalism and respect for Indian women has been depicted. Gurudatt wrote *Pathik* (1943), *Unmukta* (1944), *Swadhinta Ke Path Par* (1947), *Swaraj Dan* (1947) and many other novels numbering about one hundred. His works were merely descriptive but commercially successful. During 1937–1947 most of the above-mentioned novelists remained indifferent to the rural life.

Novels in Post-Independence Period (1947–1980)

After independence, Hindi novel-writing took a major turn. There was a phenomenal rise in the number of novelists and novels published. Most of the novelists concentrated on contemporary socio-economic and political problems and the struggles waged by the lower and lower-middle classes for a new era of development and reconstruction. There have been several kinds of contradictions in Indian society at various levels of caste and class, village and town, individual and group, cultural and political economy, etc. Some of the important novels of post-independence era, especially from 1950s to 1970s are as follows: Nagarjun's *Balchanma* (1952), Bhairav Prasad Gupta's, *Ganga Maiya* (1952) and *Sati Maiya Ka Chaura* (1959), Phanishwarnath Renu's, *Maila Anchal* (1954) and *Parati Pari Katha* (1957), Rajendra Yadav's, *Ukhare Hue Log* (1955), *Shah aur Mat*, and *Sara Akash* (1960), Amrit Roy's, *Jangal* (1969), Krishna Baldev Vaid's, *Uska Bachpan* (1957), Himansu Srivastav's, *Lohe Ke Pankh* (1957), Udai Shankar Bhatt's, *Sagar, Laheren Aur Manushya* (1956), Yashpal's, *Jhutha Sach* (Vol. I in 1958 and Vol. II in 1960), and *Meri Teri Uski Bat* (1974), Mohan Rakesh's, *Andhere Band Kamare* (1961), Shani's, *Kala Jal* (1965), Rahi Masoom Raza's, *Adha Gaon* (1966), Usha Priyamvada's, *Rukogi Nahin Radhika* (1967), Shiv Prasad Singh's, *Alag Alag Vaitarni* (1967), Jagdish Chandra's, *Dharti Dhan Na Apna* (1972) and *Kabhi Na Chhaden Khet* (1976), Bhishma Sahni's, *Tamas* (1973), Kashi Nath Singh's, *Apna Morcha* (1973), Jagdamba Prasad Dixit's, *Murda Ghar* (1974), Agyeya's, *Nadi Ke Dweep* (1951) and *Apne Apne Ajnabi* (1961), Amrit Lal Nagar's, *Bund Aur Samudra*

(1956), *Amrit Aur Vish* (1966) and *Nachyo Bahut Gopal* (1978), Krishna Sobti's, *Zindaginama*, Shrilal Shukla's, *Rag Darbari* (1967), Nirmal Varma's, *Lal Tin Ki Chhat* (1978), and *Ek Chithara Sukh* (1979), Rangeya Raghav's, *Kab Tak Pukarun* (1957), Naresh Mehta's, *Yah Path Bandhu Tha* (1962), Shailesh Matiyani's, *Sarpgandha* (1979), Viveki Roy's, *Shweta Patra* (1979), Govind Mishra's, *Lal Pili Jamin* (1976), Mannu Bhandari's, *Apka Bunty* (1971), and *Mahabhoj* (1979), Badiujjaman's, *Ek Chuhe Ki Maut* (1971), Dharmvir Bharati's, *Suraj Ka Satwan Ghora*, Mridula Garg's, *Kathgulab*, Manohar Shyam Joshi's, *Kuru Kuru Swaha* (1980), etc.

Major features of the novels written during 1950s–1970s are as follows:[29]

(a) Individualism and increasing gap between middle and lower classes are major issues of many novels of this period. For example, *Nadi Ke Dweep*, *Apne Apne Ajnabi* by Agyeya, *Suraj Ka Satwan Ghora* by Dharmvir Bharati, *Andhere Band Kamare* by Mohan Rakesh, *Shah Aur Mat* by Rajendra Yadav, and Wo Din by Nirmal Varma narrate life governed by these issues.

(b) The changing socio-economic norms, values and relationships in rural areas are reflected in novels like *Balchanma* by Nagarjun, *Ganga Maiya* by Bhairav Prasad Gupta, *Maila Anchal* by Renu, *Ukhare Hue Log* by Rajendra Yadav, *Adha Gaon* by Rahi Masoom Raza, *Amrit Aur Vish* by Amritlal Nagar, *Alag Alag Vaitarni* by Shiv Prasad Singh, *Dharti Dhan na Apna*, and *Kabhi Na Chhaden Khet* by Jagdish Chandra, *Apan Morcha* by Kashi Nath Singh and *Rag Darbari* by Shrilal Shukla.

(c) Communalism also attracted the attention of Hindi novelists in this period. For instance, one may look into *Sati Maiya Ka Chaura* by Bhairav Prasad Gupta, *Jhutha Sach* by Yashpal, *Adha Gaon* by Rahi Masoom Raza, *Alag Alag Vaitarni* by Shiv Prasad Singh, and *Tamas* by Bhishma Sahni.

(d) The policies and plans of development did not remain unnoticed by these writers. We may, for example, go through *Rag Darbari* by Shrilal Shukla in this context.

Contemporary Period

The last two decades of the twentieth century (1981–2000) and first decade of twenty-first century constitute the contemporary period. During this period, some of the important Hindi novels published are following:

Kisangarh Ke Aheri (1981), *Savdhan! Niche Aag Hai* (1986), *Dhar* (1990) *Sutradhar*, and *Jangal Jahan Shuru Hota Hai* (2000) by Sanjeev, *Darul Safa* (1981) by Raj Krishna Mishra, *Apne Apne Konark* (1995) by Chandrakanta, *Lekin Darwaja* (1982) by Pankaj Bishta, *Tatsam* (1983) by Raji Seth, *Saat Nadiyan Ek Samundar* (1984), *Shalmali* (1987), *Thikare Ki Mangani* (1989), *Zinda Muhavare* (1993), *Kuiya Jan* by Nasira Sharma, *Jhini Jhini Bini Chadaria* (1986) by Abdul Bismillah, *Ao Pepe Ghar Chalen* (1993), and *Chhinamasta* by Prabha Khetan, *Idannamam* (1994), *Chak* (1997) and *Alma Kabutari* (2000) by Maitreyi Pushpa, *Ek Zamin Apni* (1990) by Chitra Mudgal, *Doob* (1991) by Virendra Jain, *Pahi Ghar*, and *Bedakhal* by Kamla Kant Tripathi, *Yeh Jo Dilli Hai* (1993), and *Papa Ke Jane Ke Bad* (1998) by Prakash Manu, *Hamara Shahar Us Baras* (1998) by Gitanjalishri, *Parchhain Nach* (2000) by Priyamvad, *Beech Mein Vinay* (1994) by Swayam Prakash, *Sat Asman* (1996) by Asgar Wajahat, *Kalikatha via Bypass* (1998) by Alka Sarawagi, *Kal Katha* (1998) by Kamta Nath, *Mujhe Chand Chahiye* (1994), *Katna Shami Ka Vriksha Padmapankhuri Ki Dar Se* (2010) by Surendra Varma, *Narak Kund Mein Vas* (1994) by Jagdish Chandra, *Ag Pani Akash* by Ram Dhari Singh Diwakar, *Sukha Bargad* (1986) by Manjoor Ehtesham, *Trishul*, and *Akhiri Chhalang* by Shivamurti, *Adigram Upakhyan* by Kunal Singh, *Global Gaon Ke Devata* by Ranendra, *Ye Wo Sahar Nahin* by Pankaj Subir, *Prati Sansar* by Manoj Rupara, *Dukkham Sukkham* by Mamta Kalia, *Rehan Par Ragghu* by Kashinath Singh, 17, *Ranade Road* by Ravindra Kalia, *Prem Ki Bhutkatha* by Vibhuti Narayan Roy, etc.

Important features of these Hindi novels may be described as follows:[30]

(a) Diversity of social life has been accorded recognition. For example, one may go through *Jangal Jahan Shuru Hota Hai* by Sanjiv, *Narak Kund Mein Vas* by Jagdish Chandra, *Chak* by Maitreyi Pushpa, *Jhini Jhini bini Chadaria* by Abdul Bismillah and other novels. This was to refocus Premchand's tradition as a priority.

(b) Urban centres of varied sizes have been used as bases for literary creation. For instance, *Dilo Danish* (1993) and *Samay Sargam* (2000) by Krishna Sobti, *Ek Zamin Apni* (1990) by Chitra Mudgal, *Mujhe Chand Chahiye* (1993) by Surendra Varma, *Chhinnamasta* (1993) by Prabha Khetan, *Kalikatha* via *Bypass* (1998) by Alka Sarawagi, etc., are such novels.

(c) Many novels, written during this period, are centred on women's issues. Discourse on women (*Stree vimarsh*) has been one of the main themes of this period. *Yuddhasthal* (1981) by Mithileshwar, *Tumhari Roshani Mein* (1985) by Govind Mishra, *Yamini Katha* (1991) by Suryabala, *Apne Apne Konark* (1995) by Chandrakanta, *Shalmali* (1987) by Naisra Sharma, *Kathgulab* (1986) by Mridula Garg, *Ardhanarishwar* (1993) by Vishnu Prabhakar, *Alma Kabutari* (2000), *Chak* (1997), and *Idannamam* (1994) by Maitreyi Pushpa, *Aao Pepe Ghar Chalen* (1990) and *Chhinnamasta* (1993) by Prabha Khetan, *Ek Zamin Apni* (1990) and *Awan* by Chitra Mudgal, *Mujhe Chand Chahiye* (1993) by Surendra Varma, *Dilo Danish* (1993) by Krishna Sobti.

(d) During this period dalit life also got prominent space in Hindi novels. Discourse on Dalits (*dalit vimarsh*) is one of main currents of Hindi literature. For example, these are *Narak Kund Mein Vas* (1994) by Jagdish Chandra, *Shailush* (1989) by Shiv Prasad Singh, *Alma Kabutari* by Maitreyi Pushpa, *Yatha Prastavit* (1982), and *Parishishta* (1984) by Giriraj Kishor, *Kissa Gulam* (1986) by Ramesh Chandra Shah, etc. Dalit community was also represented by writers from within. Jai Prakash Kardam, a dalit writer, wrote *Chhappar* (1994), and Ajay Navaria wrote *Udhar Ke Log*.

(e) Communalism continued to be an important issue in Hindi novels during this period; for instance, we may see *Shahar Mein Curfew* (1998) by Vibhuti Narayan Roy, *Shirshak* (1996) by Chandra Kishore Jaiswal, *Sukha Bargad* (1986) by Manzoor Ehtesham, Zinda Muhavare (1993) by Nasira Sharma, *Sabha Parv* (1994) by Badiuzama, *Unmad* (1999) by Bhagwan Singh, *Hamara Shahar Us Baras* (1998) by Gitanjalishri, etc.

(f) The activities and machinations of those engaged in politics also attracted the attention of active writers of this period, For instance, there are *Darul Safa* (1981) by Raj Krishna Mishra, *Kissa Loktanatra* (1993) by V.N. Roy, *Bishrampur Ka Sant* (1998) by Shrilal Shukla, *Jangal Jahan Shuru Hota Hai* (2000) by Sanjeev, etc.

(g) The problems of Indians in foreign countries and events of international importance have also been taken up as themes for writing novels in this period. For example, in *Do Desh Aur Tisari Udasi* (1997) Mahendra Bhalla depicts the problem of migrant Indians in England, especially the problem of racism. Similarly, Nasira Sharma wrote the novel *Sat Nadiyan Ek Samundar* (1984) about modern Iran's Islamic revolution. Further, Prabha Khetan wrote *Ao Pepe Ghar Chalen* in 1990 about the alienation faced by American women despite all sorts of material comforts. Mridula Garg also wrote *Kathgulab* (1996) about women's problems in America. Giriraj Kishor has written a novel on Mahatma Gandhi, while, he was struggling in South Africa with the problem of racism, under the title *Pahala Girmitiya* (1999).

(h) There has been a trend of dealing with individual fear, disappointment, insecurity, etc., in some of the novels of the last two decades of the twentieth century; for instance, *Rat Ka Reporter* (1980), and *Antim Aranya* (2000) by Nirmal Varma, *Kuru Kuru Swaha* (1980), and *Haria Hercules Ki Hairani* (1996) by Manohar Shyam Joshi, *Kihlega to Dekhenge* (1996) and *Deevar Mein Khidki Rehti Thi* by Vinod Kumar Shukla, *Gujara Hua Zamana* (1981), *Nar Nari* (1996) and *Maya Lok* (1999) by Krishna Baldev Vaid, *Parchhain Nach* (2000) by Priyamvad.

Thus, one finds many strands in Hindi novel-writing. The above-mentioned issues indicate the widening of the aperture of literary mind.

Dalits and Dalit Literature

The term 'dalit' is not very clear and specific. In its narrow sense, it refers to the ex-untouchables only while in its wider sense it connotes to all the deprived, depressed and oppressed castes (including other backward classes) in India. However, there are four major terms concerned with the dalits' identity. These are explained below:

(a) *'Achhut'* or *'Asprishya'* (untouchables): Under this category, all those castes and sub-castes were included who were not allowed to touch the members of upper caste Hindus; water was not accepted from their hands, they were not allowed to directly participate in religious functions and were not allowed even the temple entry.

(b) Next identity emerged during early twentieth century when M.K. Gandhi addressed them as *'harijans'* (sons of God). When Gandhi actively joined the freedom struggle in early twentieth century, he found that Indians were very much divided on caste lines and caste Hindus were discriminating against the untouchables and were also inhumanly treating the latter. He began a reform movement for their amelioration through change of heart, and in the process decided to call them *'harijans'*. However, for Gandhi, attaining national freedom was the primary goal and emancipation of dalits was a secondary problem and could be solved after attaining freedom.

(c) B.R. Ambedkar was not happy with Gandhiji's moderate stand nor with his nomenclature of *'harijan'*. He addressed the untouchables as the 'depressed' or 'dalits' who were oppressed both socially and economically. Ambedkar was of the view that the dalits were original inhabitants of India but were conquered by the Aryans who made them their slaves and declared them as the untouchables. To him, dalit problem was not a problem of Hindus, but that of the entire nation. Unlike

Gandhiji, he wanted that without solving the dalit problem, the issue of national independence could not be sorted out, hence he wanted a separate electorate for dalits – but ultimately compromised with Gandhi's view of inclusion of all as voters even for the election of dalits under Poona Pact.[31]

(d) The British government had categorised many lowly castes under the rubric of 'depressed castes' and later they were categorised by the Government of India after independence as Scheduled Castes (SCs).

Dalits are basically the ex-untouchables covered by the term Scheduled Castes (as declared by the Government of India through a gazette), not including Scheduled Tribes (STs), Other Backward Classes (OBCs) and caste Hindus. The term 'dalit', however, connotes all those at the lowest rung of Hindu social hierarchical order where Brahmins are at the top, followed by Kshatriyas, Vaishyas, Shudras and finally dalits (who are also called 'Panchams' as they do not fit in the four varna system). Needless to say that varna is textual (in theory) while caste is contextual (in practice). However, there is a difference of emphasis in the meanings of the terms '*Achhut*', '*Harijan*', 'Scheduled Caste' and 'dalit'. While '*Achhut*' was considered both by outsiders as well as the community insiders as unintelligent and inhuman (hence exclusion from mainstream), the term '*harijan*' brought a moderate position (reformative inclusion) and finally the term 'dalit' brought a sense of conscious and rebel character (self-assertion, self-confidence and self-recognition), hence asserted 'reinclusion' on the one hand and threat of 'potential self-exclusion' (to discard Hinduism) on the other. Further, while *Achhuts* were exploited by the upper caste Hindus as well as Muslims 'by force' (the process of dominance), Harijans more or less accepted the customs and traditions of the upper caste Hindus and followed the upper castes through a process of 'sanskritisation' (to use M.N. Srinivas' term) 'by consent' (the hegemony); the dalits at present have challenged and questioned the traditional social hierarchy of Hinduism itself and they want to replace the vertical order (of inequality) by a horizontal order (of equality). Thus, with the new awakening of dalits, there has emerged 'dalit literature' also. We would discuss it below.

Under the leadership of B.R. Ambedkar, several Marathi dalit writers such as Bandhu Madhav, Baburao Babul, Shankarrao Kharat, Annu Bhau Sathe, Keshav Meshram, Yogiraj Wagmere, Yogendra Meshram, Daya Pawar, Sharat Kumar Limbale, etc., have established their names in Marathi literature. Most of them wrote their experiences, as did Ambedkar. This tradition was also planted in Hindi literature, especially during the last two decades of the twentieth century. Now, the fundamental questions have been raised: who is a dalit writer and what is a 'dalit creation'? There are mainly three views on the issue:

(a) Most of the dalits such as Jai Prakash Kardam, Mohandas Naimish Rai, Dr N. Singh, C.B. Bharti, etc., are of the view that only someone who is a 'born dalit' (ex-untouchable) can really write dalit literature because of direct self-experience (*swanubhuti*) and others cannot produce real dalit literature because they have no direct dalit-experience. As non-dalits' writings about dalits are not considered authentic due to 'sympathy' (*sahanubhuti*), hence these cannot be categorised as dalits' creation.

(b) There are some other writers, especially from backward classes/castes, who want a broader forum or organisation or organisational front of dalit and backward writers in order to challenge the so-called hegemony of Upper Caste writers. Rajendra Yadav, Ramanika Gupta, Prem Kumar Mani, Madhukar Singh, Purushottam Agrawal, Mudra Rakshas, etc., are of this view. However, some of dalit writers do not accept writers from backward castes as belonging to their dalit fold because the latter are not born dalits. Further it is feared that they would grab the opportunities meant for dalit writers leaving them deprived.

(c) Most of the famous Hindi writers do not accept such categories as 'dalit literature' and 'dalit writers'; for instance, Namvar Singh Ram Darash Mishra, Doodh Nath Singh, Shailesh Matiyani, Kashi Nath Singh, Swayam Prakash, etc., are of this view. Kashi Nath Singh once said: "to write on dalits one need not be a dalit .... There are dalit writers in Hindi but not dalit literature."[32] Ram Darash Mishra also wrote: "Reservation in the literature cannot work and even the group noise cannot make literature."[33] Shailesh Matiyani was of the similar view: "to appreciate petty writings and creations too much means closing the possibilities of the future."[34] Doodh Nath Singh also remarked: "The question of quality does not arise if one accepts that only a born dalit can be a dalit writer. Then it is only a category."[35] A noted sociologist Prof K.L. Sharma (2011) talks of 'social difference' and 'power' as most effective bases of social stratification. To him, caste as a system has lost its appeal but caste as a phenomenon has gained considerable space in elections, mobilisations and in extra-legal actions. Hence, he finds caste more as an identity rather than a bedrock of intercaste and intracaste relations. Therefore dalit writers should not take a parochial and biased approach of dalit literature being 'of dalits, for dalits and by dalits.'

However, some dalit writers have asserted that dalit literature has its own aesthetics. A dalit writer, C.B. Bharti, has noted the following features of aesthetics of dalit literature in Hindi:[36]

(a) Whereas the aesthetics of Hindi literature is dominated by the considerations of 'satya' (truth), 'shiv' (welfare) and 'sundar' (beautiful), dalit literature goes beyond artistry and literariness by emphasising more on 'content' than on the form. Thus, dalit literature expresses hatred against the mainstream cultural tradition of the upper caste Hindus and questions various sorts of exploitation of dalits.

(b) Dalit literature questions religious faith and spirituality, gods and goddesses, superstitions, etc., prevalent in Hinduism and it bases mostly on 'inner-inspiration'.

(c) It focuses more on the utility of a particular thing and, therefore, following utilitarian principle of Socrates, to dalit writers, most of the mainstream Hindi literature is useless and worthless.

(d) Dalits consider that considerations of aesthetics may be both objective and subjective. The same thing may be beautiful for one person but ugly for the other.

(e) Dalits accept only that literature as dalit literature, which is written by a dalit writer and is about dalits. 'Self-experience' of a 'born dalit' makes his/her writings most realistic and authentic. Therefore, dalit writers claim to have succeeded in depicting quite realistically the life and living conditions chiefly through autobiographies.

(f) Dalit aesthetics emphasises rigorously on equality, liberty and fraternity rather than what dalits call artificial propositions or traditions of mainstream aesthetics. Therefore, their language is more direct, simple, rough and aggressive.

(g) Dalit writers have taken their inspiration from B.R. Ambedkar, Gautam Buddha, Guru Ravidas, Jyotiba Phule, Sri Narayana Guru, E.V. Ramaswamy Naikar and Swami Achhutanand who dedicated their lives before for the establishment of an egalitarian ideology, culture and society.

However, such contention is not widely accepted because, as Ajay Tiwari rightly observes: real situation, ideal perspective and romantic emotion are interrelated in literature, though independent but not inimical and fully autonomous. Since any ideology of idealism is the hyperbolic form of reality, hence we may call it "maximum form of reality".[37] The relevance of realism lies in its trend and mode to explore various layers, diversities, interconnections and contradictions of reality. Realism is to change the objectivity to a conscious directional dynamics. To reflect reality means the internalisation of the external and to create reality means the externalisation of the internal, as Gajanan Madhav Muktibodh used to observe. Ernest Fischer rightly observes:

"Realism is determined partly by private and partly by social perspective of the artist."[38] Hence, in realism, individual artist's class position, context, pressure of tradition, emotions, inner world, and experience are reflected in a combined way.

Thus, from the above, we get a brief sketch of the rise of Hindi novel, and the carving out of space for dalit characters therein. Now, the question of sociological theories of literature arises. We will discuss this in the next chapter.

Notes and References

1. Karl Mannheim (1982), 'Sociology of Knowledge', in J.E. Curtis and J.W. Petras (eds.), *Sociology of Knowledge: A Reader*, G. Duckworth and Company Limited, London, p. 110.
2. Ibid., p. 111.
3. Ibid., p. 118.
4. Ibid., pp. 118–19.
5. Ibid., p. 121.
6. J.E. Curtis and J.W. Petras (1952), 'Introduction', in J.E. Curtis and J.W. Petras (eds.), *Sociology of Knowledge: A Reader*, G. Duckworth and Company Limited, London, p. 3.
7. I. Watt (1957), *The Rise of the Novel*, The University of California Press, Berkeley, p. 11.
8. J. Leenhardt (1977), 'The Sociology of Literature: Some Stages in its History', in J. Routh and J. Wolff (eds.), *The Sociology of Literature*, University of Keele, Keele, p. 531.
9. Milan Kundera (1992), *The Art of the Novel*, Rupa & Co., Calcutta (now Kolkata), pp. 4–5.
10. Ibid., p. 4.
11. Ibid., p. 14.
12. Ibid., p. 137.
13. Ibid., p. 139.
14. Ibid., p. 143.
15. Ibid., p. 142.
16. Ralph Fox (1956), *The Novel and the People*, Foreign Language Publishing House, Moscow, p. 72.

17. Bharat Bhushan Agrawal (1971), *Hindi Upanayas Par Paschatya Prabhav*, R.C. Jain Evam Santati, Delhi, p. 34.
18. E.M. Forster (1982), *Upanyas Ke Paksha* (Hindi translation of 'Aspects of Novel'), Rajasthan Hindi Granth Akademi, Jaipur, p. 16.
19. Gopal Roy (2002), *Hindi Upanyas Ka Itihas*, Rajkamal Prakashan, New Delhi, p. 27.
20. Gopal Roy (1968), *Hindi Upanyas Kosh*, Vol. I, Granth Niketan, Patna, p. 34.
21. Ibid., p. 35.
22. See Gopal Roy (2002), op. cit., p. 44.
23. Kunwar Pal Singh (1976), *Hindi Upanyas: Samajik Chetna*, Pandulipi Prakashan, Delhi, pp. 23–24.
24. Gopal Roy (2002), op. cit., p. 65.
25. Ibid., p. 42.
26. K.P. Singh (1976), op. cit., pp. 150–58, see also Gopal Roy (2002), op. cit., pp. 64–67.
27. Gopal Roy (2002), op. cit., pp. 121–25.
28. Ibid., p. 165.
29. K.P. Singh (1976), op. cit., pp. 150–58.
30. Gopal Roy (2002), op. cit., pp. 399–470.
31. Kanwal Bharati (1997), *Dr Ambedkar: Ek Punarmulyankan*, Bodhisatva Prakashan, Rampur (UP), p. 15.
32. *Amar Ujala* (Hindi Daily), Meerut, dated 26 February 1996.
33. *Rashtriya Sahara* (Hindi Daily), New Delhi, dated 26 November 1992.
34. N. Singh (2002), 'Vivadon Ke Ghere Mein Dalit Sahitya', *Dalit Sahitya*, No. 4, p. 53.
35. Ibid.
36. C.B. Bharti (1996), 'Dalit Sahitya Ka Saundarya Shastra', *Yuddharat Aam Admi*, No. 34–35, April–September, pp. 56–59.
37. Ajay Tiwari (2011), 'Adarsh, Roman Aur Yatharth Ki Parasparta', *Naya Gyanodaya*, April.
38. Ernest Fischer (1971), *The Necessity of Art*, Penguin, London.

2

Dalits and Dalit Literature

Some Critical Issues

Various sociologists have underlined the relationship between literature and society through mediation in different ways. Adorno emphasised more on aesthetics while Herbert Marcuse focused on philosophical dimensions of existence. Leo Lowenthal views literature as a historical store of individual experiences that are influenced by social contexts. To him, the life experiences gained from literature are both individual as well as socio-historical, as a writer either supports or opposes the historical conditions of his time and place. He also valued the popular literature. Unlike empiricists, he does not propose a sociology of production and distribution nor accepts literature as an institution. He focuses on class basis of text under production aspect, social context under distribution aspect, and readers' reception to the text under consumption aspect. Lucien Goldmann emphasises on world vision that is inherent in the life of social class but is expressed in philosophy, art and literature only. Therefore, according to him, the search for world vision begins in the study of a text, not in the study of a class. But he has not given due importance to the author who is simply a medium (for him). But, in practice, a writer's understanding, vision and stand has a significant bearing on the depiction of social reality.

The terms 'dalit' and 'dalit literature' are highly contentious and controversial. What is a dalit literature? Its answer depends more on the perspective and attitude of the replier (subjectivity) than on the objectivity. Om Prakash Valmiki, a dalit Hindi writer, in his book *Dalit Sahitya Ka Saundarya Shashtra*[1] (Aesthetics of Dalit Literature), propounds that the situations of uncertainty in the minute wearing of idealism strengthen only the status quoism and the masks of idealism desharpen the struggle for fundamental change. There he criticises various critics of Hindi literature to whom to be a born dalit is not mandatory for writing dalit literature. He quotes Kashinath Singh: "To write about horse, one need not be a horse". But he disagrees with Singh saying that one may write about outer features of a horse (gait, organs of body, buttocks, voice) only, not his tiredness, hunger, thirst, pain and feelings about his master – these are exclusively in the internal domain of the horse. However, Valmiki escapes from answering the key question: how will the horse express himself? Similarly, how can an illiterate person express his feelings in writing? Though, at least theoretically, one may say that even an illiterate person may express orally (oral tradition is rich in the forms of folk songs, folk dances, puzzles, sayings, etc.), yet it is further relevant to ask why most of the literate persons don't write creatively or why most of the illiterate persons don't express orally? These questions clearly indicate that literature primarily requires a certain kind and level of creativity and artistry, which is usually not expressed by all human beings.

However, for elaboration, Valmiki further quotes S.S. Bechain, "Dalit is one who has been given the status of a scheduled caste",[2] But Kanwal Bharti goes one step further "Dalit is one upon whom the rule of untouchability has been imposed, who is compelled to do hard and dirty work; who was prevented from getting education and doing independent profession and upon whom the touchables imposed the code of disabilities: herein only those castes are included who are called Scheduled Castes".[3] Mohan Das Naimishrai thinks dalits to be almost equivalent to Marx's proletariat, but he finds the term 'dalit' broader as it includes social, religious, economic and political exploitation, whereas the term 'proletariat' is limited to only economic exploitation, Therefore, to him, the proletariat is basically the victim of economic inequality, whereas dalit is basically the victim of social inequality. Thus, dalits are those who are on the lowest ladder of a hierarchical social system. Narayan Surve, a Marathi dalit poet, broadens the term 'dalit' by including not only Bauddha or backward castes, but also all the victims. Another dalit Marathi writer, Baburao Bagul, thinks that the term dalit signifies revolution. To social scientist E. Zelliot, the term 'dalit' implies, "those who have been broken, ground down by those who are above them in a deliberate and active way. There is in the word itself an inherent denial of pollution, karma and justified caste hierarchy".[4] To Rajendra Yadav, in addition to untouchables, even women and backward castes are also dalits. But S.S. Bechain disagrees with him: "By this (including women and backwards) the correct picture does not emerge in the literature. Dalit literature is the literature of those untouchables who do not get respect socially. The harassment of those, who are victims of caste discrimination at social level, is expressed in to words and is becoming dalit literature".[5] Similarly, another dalit writer Kanwal Bharti defines dalit literature as one in which "dalits have themselves expressed their pain whatsoever reality dalits have experienced in their life struggle, dalit literature is a literature in that expression. It is not an art for art's sake but literature for life and desire to live. So, needless to say, in reality, only the literature written by dalits forms the category of dalit literature".[6] Again another dalit writer, C.B. Bharti defines it in this way: "It is a broad, scientific, realistic, sensitive literary intervention. Whatsoever logical, scientific, free from the prejudices of tradition is literary creation, we call it dalit literature".[7] Further to Baburao Bagul, "Dalit literature is the literature that accepts the liberation of man, that accepts man as great and that opposes the greatness of dynasty, varna and caste".[8]

O.P. Valmiki criticises two categories of non-dalit writers' views regarding dalit literature. First view does not accept the existence of dalit literature – thus it is biased with anti-dalit varna-caste mentality. Second view accepts the existence of dalit literature but opines that its forefathers/leaders were 'savarnas' (higher caste Hindus). To him, the second category is more dangerous than the first, because it does not think that it is essential for dalit writings to be done by a dalit born writer. Similarly, he also criticises a section of dalit writers who consider dalit literature as disgraceful because by writing autobiographies, dalit writers are expressing themselves – these autobiographies entertain the non-dalit readers, on the one hand, and create inferiority complex among the dalits, on the other. But, Valmiki calls them 'Brahmanic dalits' who grab the benefits of reservation provided under Indian Constitution due to the efforts of B.R. Ambedkar – they compete to become 'Brahmans' and their ideational infertility makes them opportunists. To him, dalit writers took inspiration from the autobiography of B.R. Ambedkar *Me Kasa Jhalo* (How I was made) and developed the genre of autobiography that showed the mirror of society. Therefore, he is of the opinion that dalit writers should make a thorough study of the available non-dalit literature despite disagreement and ideological opposition, only then can they reach at certain conclusions. Second, dalit literature should stand like a hard wall against injustice, exploitation, oppression and social inequalities; only then its social responsibility and ideological commitment would be proved.

Thus, most of dalit writers consider dalit literature as one written by dalits themselves. To put it differently, it is a literature 'of dalits, for dalits and by dalits'! However, both terms dalit and dalit literature, are contentious. The term 'dalit' is a generalistic category but in reality an identity is rooted in history as a 'specific' category, not as a general category. In India, it is historically proved that 'specific identities' (in terms of sub-caste, community, residence, dynasty, language, etc.) have existed. Therefore, 'dalit' as an umbrella term for all Scheduled Castes does not fit in the actual social reality. Second, there has been major social changes in terms of 'upward' and 'downward' mobility amongst various castes. Some untouchable castes, in due course of history, were accepted as 'savarna' and, on the other hand, some upper castes lost their prestige and position in the caste/varna hierarchy. For instance, Nadars in Tamil Nadu and Edawas in Kerala took the benefit of upward mobility and discarded their previous untouchable status. Similarly, in South Bihar (now Jharkhand) and Bengal, Cheros and Bhuians became Rajputs in early 19th century. Here, the lesson learnt is that if an untouchable caste discards its traditional (dirty) occupation and takes up modern occupation, it improves economic status and is linked to the power structure – its social status may change from the untouchable to the touchable one. Third, there occur intra-dalit conflicts due to oppositional interests between different ex-untouchable sub-castes (due to specific identities). A cobbler boy would not like to freely mix-up (sitting and dining together) with a sweeper boy, not to say of intermarrying between these two specific dalit sub-castes. Fourth, for taking benefit of protective discrimination (reservation of jobs, seats in educational institutions, stipend, etc.) most of the ex-untouchables use their 'specific identity' (sub-caste) and after taking the benefit, talk of 'general dalit identity' elsewhere, thus there exists some kind of ambivalence and dualism on the part of most of dalits in this regard. Fifth, it is not true that these dalits have always been the sufferers and deprived in every way in all aspects in all regions in India: for example, Dusadhs in North Bihar, Bhars/Rajbhars in eastern U.P., Cheros and Bandhawats in Chhotanagpur (Jharkhand) and others in different parts of India in medieval period have been the rulers. Finally, it is also evident in different parts of India that after taking the benefit of protective discrimination, many of the dalits with higher prestige/post try to distance themselves from their community masses (both general and specific identities) on the one hand, and try to be closer to the elites of the upper castes on the other, due to some form of 'sanskritisation'. This tendency also falsifies the generalistic dalit identity.

As far as the issue of dalit literature is concerned, the position taken by most of the dalit writers 'of, for and by the dalits' is also not acceptable because of following reasons:

In O.P. Valmiki's view, dalit literature has following features:

(a) Dalit literature requires a separate aesthetics and it will add to the aesthetics of Hindi literature. Dalit literature is a 'literature of negation', born from the struggle and revolt and there is equality, freedom and fraternity, on the one hand, and opposition to caste and varna,[9] on the other.

(b) It is optimistic for a better life in future, despite adverse circumstances – it is a 'literature of future'.[10]

(c) Earlier, during Bhakti movement period there were saint poets from amongst dalits, but they had no dalit consciousness for social change. Similarly, during 1960–90 some dalit writers were active with a class perspective, away from the caste/varna struggle, and they were day dreaming without real dalit concerns, hence their writings don't fit in dalit literature.[11] Dalit consciousness requires acceptance of B.R. Ambedkar's philosophy, Buddha's atheism and non-existence of soul, and opposition to feudalism, Brahmanism and communalism.[12] It tries to redefine the ideals and outcomes of Hindi literature.[13]

(d) Self-experience is the key to dalit literature-expression without fetters. It emphasises on the intention and content of writing, not the form and style. It negates imaginary standards.[14]

(e) In dalit literature there is not merely a copy of reality but realistic re-creation of ordinary characters in ordinary circumstances.[15] Here philosophical and artistic show is not needed.

(f) Dalit writers struggle on two fronts: first, their poverty-ridden settlements and darkness therein; second, the outer system that has poisoned their life through social inequalities and discrimination.[16]

(g) Dalit literature is against the incarnation of gods and god-like heroes who are protectors of Brahmans, but anti-women and anti-dalit, they are war-lovers. It treats past as a black chapter. Hence dalit literature focuses on the greatness of every individual.[17] It re-establishes Karna, Shambuk and Eklavya as true heroes who were ill-treated in mainstream literature.

(h) Dalit literature criticises the inegalitarian land distribution[18] and related issues like Panchayati Raj system, which in the view of Ambedkar, is 'the workshop of casteism and varna system'.

(i) Dalit literature negates sanskritised language and its poetics rather it uses easy and simple Hindi language, which is used by the common people in everyday life. Dalit literature does not mind using abuses and bitter words – it negates the traditional principles of 'purity' and 'greatness' in literature because it considers purity and greatness principles in language as artificial and elitist.[19]

These points, however, are more polemical than analytical. Here our contention is as follows: First, as Marx and George Lukacs have rightly observed that a top rate literary production is done only when the writer transcends his class. This is to say, he has to 'declass' himself. In Indian context, in addition, it is required of a writer to 'decaste' himself, as in western context it is required of him to 'derace' himself. It is very interesting to note that most of dalit writers criticise non-dalit writers for being biased, for seeing thing 'from above', for justifying the hierarchical varna/caste system, therefore they demand, in different ways, that non-dalit writers should 'decaste' themselves in order to grasp the nuances of dalit experience as well as dalit perspective. But, unfortunately, they themselves do not 'decaste', rather they portray one-sided hyperbolic, narrow and limited picture of social reality and experience. Thus, most of dalit writers practice 'reverse caste discrimination'.

Second, if non-dalits' writings are condemned on superficial grounds (say, the use of term 'Chamar' by Premchand in his novel *Rangbhumi* led to the burning of this significant social novel by several dalit writers in 2004 in Delhi) or on the grounds that non-dalits have no moral right to write about dalits, dalit literature being the privilege and 'exclusive copy right' of the dalits – the domain of dalit literature would be narrower, limited, one-dimensional, uncritical and non-creative due to lack of dialogue between different conflicting views/perspectives. And thus, this tendency is highly harmful to the literary creation in general and to dalit literature in particular.

Third, most of the dalit literature is limited to autobiographies (and to some extent stories) based on childhood experience of several decades long long ago. Thus, instead of portraying the contemporary socio-economic and political reality realistically, they depict outdated so-called self-experiences.

Fourth, with a narrow and limited world-view, Hindi dalit writers have not been able to write quality literature in general and quality novels in particular; as a novel depicts the whole life in an era, most of dalit writers have not been successful in depicting a great novel. Different characters speak differently on a specific issue as happens in true life-situations. As a noted critic Ian Watts rightly observes that reality lies in the way in which a novel presents the kind of life ('how' rather than 'what'). But most of dalit literature does not go beyond 'what'.

Fifth, most of dalit writers focus on caste as 'a prime mover of social behaviour', 'a powerful force conditioning social mindset of dalits' (Punalekar). Thus for them caste is an all-pervasive institution – it determines the position and direction of Hindu society, hence the entire society is subsumed by the caste, and other aspects like economic, political and cultural are secondary and subsidiary to the caste. But it is not true historically. Sometimes political factor, sometimes cultural factor, sometimes economic factor and sometimes social (caste) factor, or more than one factor, becomes decisive in Indian society. Actually, there lies a dynamic and dialectical relationship between these facets of life. Therefore, dalits' view of caste determinism (society in caste) is not always tenable in practice. Many dalit writers like Baburao Bagul are of the view that in India the Hindu view of life is all-pervasive, even non-Hindus' (Christians, Muslims, Sikh, Bauddhas, Jains, etc.) mentality is likewise believing in soul, rebirth, sin, reincarnation, etc. Hence they declare the entire Indian literature as 'Hindu literature'.[20] Bagul further observes: "Power-struggle, victory-defeat, sublimation of the victorious and devilisation of the defeated is the specificity of the culture and literature of Hindu society".[21] He further adds that the form of Indian democracy is ordinarily casteist, a caste in majority rules in an area and once reaching the top of the political power, that caste finds the power of religion conducive. He observes: "Those who see the sorrow, providers of sorrow and the guardians of sorrow-givers, their writings were expressed in the form of 'parallel literature' in Hindi. It is strange that 'dalit literature' in Marathi and 'parallel literature' in Hindi came at the same time".[22]

But these observations are not fully correct. In fact, the entire Indian literature is not Hindu literature. There have always been different types of Hindi literature and the 'parallel literature' (especially stories of Rajendra Yadav, Kamleshwar, Mohan Rakesh and Madhukar Singh) has been different from the mainstream literature. Two verses from Sanskrit literature, the classical ancient language of India, also support my point: First verse says: Let all be happy, let all be disease-free, let all see ...

> Sarve Bhavantu Sukhinah, Sarve Santu Niramayah,
> Sarve Bhadrani Pashyantu, Ma Kashchit dukh bhagbhaveta.

Second verse says:

> Ayam Nijah Parovetti Gadna Laghuchetsam,
> Udar charitanam tu vasudhaiva kutumbakam.

(This is mine, that is yours, is the tendency of a small person; to great persons the entire earth is their family). Further an ancient book 'Vajrasuchi' (by Aswaghosh) written in Sanskrit has been quite revolutionary and liberating.

These two Sanskrit verses composed in ancient period clearly see all as human beings only, not as 'we' versus 'they'. That is, there is neither religious consideration nor caste consideration, neither power struggle nor victory-defeat consideration. No doubt, there has been caste discrimination in India in theory and practice, yet caste does not encompass everything. Had the society been absolutely rigid, how there were processes of upward and downward mobility in the caste hierarchy, change of castes, emergence of new castes in an era and disappearance of old castes in another and different status of different castes in different parts of India (in some parts higher status, in other parts lower status). Further some ancient scriptures like Manusmriti talked of discrimination in the arena of occupation, education, law, economy and polity on the basis of varna but varna was textual while caste was contextual.

Sixth, it is not out of context to mention here that most of dalit writers are intolerant to others writing about dalits. Though some of the dalit characters of Premchand (say Ghisu-Madhav in his story 'Kafan') have not struggled and revolted against the prevailing system, yet his other dalit characters (like Surdas in his novel *Rangbhumi* or Siliya in *Godan*, or dalit woman in *Ghaswali*) have taken a strong stand against exploitation of various sorts ranging from individual to gender, from community to the nation. One cannot forget the fighting spirit of Surdas against the colonial system, bureaucracy and capitalistic industrialisation. He fully understands that he lost the struggle because of disunity against the united enemies (British empire and Indian capitalist class) but he declares to fight again and again unitedly as well as reconstruct his hut again and again. Thus, Surdas is like modern Raidas (respected by all). Premchand took a stand for dalits' all-round liberation (social, economic and political) and went beyond treating them sympathetically, rather applied empathy. But Premchand too was marked by limitations of that era, and this has to be kept in mind to be fair to him. As Sadanand Shahi rightly observes: "It was not Premchand's fault that by his age Kabir had reached there to give consolation to Ghisu-Madhav (of 'Kafan' story), not Ambedkar. Therefore, it seems to me that protest to 'Kafan' (by dalit writers) means protest to Kabir".[23]

Seventh, dalit literature, especially in Hindi, has been less creative, artistic and imaginative rather more vocal, bold and aggressive. The so-called self-experience pervades at the cost of creativity and aesthetics. Often populistic slogans, abuses, emotional outbursts, opposition for opposition sake, revengeful depiction of upper caste characters, fatwas to non-dalit characters, repetition, depiction of outdated practices as present ones and thus, these dalit writers make dalit literature more a 'natural stock' or 'raw materials' of sociology than artistic literary creation. As Manager Pandey perceptively remarks. "Literature is an art and it takes time to mature. Having feeling is not enough .... The quality of literature that has a tradition of five thousand years can not be sought in the literature of dalits that has barely any past. On the other hand, the dalit should understand that literature is an art".[24] Further, Lowenthal in his three books *Literature, Popular Culture and Society*, *Literature and Image of Man*, and *The Art of Narrative and Society* rightly emphasises that in creative literature, experience of reality and a perspective to it is more significant than depiction of reality. He rightly disagreed with Walter Benjamin's observation that in history only the voice of the victorious are expressed – to him, actually in a true art, often the voice of the defeated and desire of their victory are expressed in history.

Eighth, most of dalit writers have a limited vision and world-view, hence they write/publish second rate autobiographies or third rate novels. O.P. Valmiki's *Juthan* is a third rate autobiography but it got undeserving publicity inside and outside India due to media hype and promotion by some western scholars with an imperialistic view of dividing Indian writers on the basis of caste. Thus, though there is more public space for dalit writers (many journals have fixed columns for dalit discourse, or have published special issues on dalits like 'Hans' and 'Kathadesh') yet there is no depth. Actually, any creative literature requires "internal, essential and indivisible unity between form and content" (Lowenthal), but most of dalit writers harp on content at the cost of form.

Ninth, most of dalit writers have deliberately ignored the intra-caste conflict and gender conflicts among dalits in their writings, because then they would be exposed from within at various levels. Dalit writers like Dharmvir have been anti-dalit women due to his feudal mentality to condemn dalit women. But Kaushalya Vaishyantri ('Dohra Abhishap') has shown that dalit woman also suffers from male chauvinism at the hands of dalits themselves. Actually, a dalit woman has triple curses: economic (poverty), social (untouchability) and gender (patriarchy).

Tenth, most of the dalit writers are intolerant to criticism and are 'victims of immediacy' ('here and now' – as phenomenologists call it). They are almost blind followers of dalit politicians (especially B.R. Ambedkar), hence their thinking and understanding is not broadened. A revolutionary writer shows the way to the politicians and others (literature as a guide) but dalit writers have been playing a role secondary to dalit politicians. They are victims of 'identity politics' too, but in reality national culture remains always greater than the sum total of sub-cultures (identities), though I recognise the free play of great/national and local/little cultures at a given place and time, both having autonomous as well as interdependent spheres.

Finally, as I have shown elsewhere in detail after analysing four Hindi novels (by Premchand, Ugra, Giriraj Kishore and Jagdish Chandra) to realistically depict dalit characters in a novel, it does not seem to be necessary for the writer to be a born dalit. Rather his world vision and the capacity to empathise with the dalits by transcending his social (caste) and economic (class) backgrounds can prove to be helpful for enabling him in carrying out his mission.[25] Actually, certain kinds of mediation are required for depiction. That is why, Raymond Williams emphasises on social totality, mediation and hegemony. His 'cultural materialism' focuses more on generation than on social structure, community than class, and experience than ideology.

However, to be fair, one may say that dalit writing is a facet of a broader democratisation of Hindi literature in terms of number, voice of dissent/other, and coverage of some unexplored areas. The inclusiveness and perspective from below is leading towards a new social process of creativity with a paradigm shift from 'objects of writing' to 'subjects of writing'. This is an appreciable tendency but they should not only welcome and tolerate criticism from outside (non-dalits) but should also do introspection and self-criticism so that a matured and critical dalit-writing may flourish in Hindi literature. Dalit writers have to broaden their perception about non-dalits writing about dalits, because ultimately the range and depth of art matters the most in creative writing, in the interest of the dalits as well as Hindi literature. Actually, following Mikhail Bakhtin, we may conclude that neither the internal world of the creative writing is fully self-dependent nor fully dependent on external world, rather the dichotomy of internal and external worlds is false. The dialogical language, creative communication and imagination are the essential pillars of creative literature, but unfortunately most of dalit literature lacks these qualities.

References

1. O.P. Valmiki (2001), *Dalit Sahitya Ka Saundarya Shastra*, Radhakrishna Prakashan Pvt. Ltd., New Delhi.
2. Ibid., p. 13.
3. Ibid., p. 13.
4. E. Zelliot (1996), *From Untouchable to Dalit*, Manohar Publications, New Delhi, p. 267.
5. Cited in O. P. Valmiki, op. cit., p. 15.
6. Ibid., pp. 14–15.
7. Ibid., p. 15.
8. Ibid., p. 16.
9. Ibid., p. 16.
10. Ibid., p. 21.
11. Ibid., p. 30.
12. Ibid., p. 31.
13. Ibid., p. 33.

14. Ibid., p. 50.
15. Ibid., p. 59.
16. Ibid., p. 68.
17. Ibid., p. 74.
18. Ibid., p. 79.
19. Ibid., p. 81.
20. Baburao Bagul (2003), "Dalit Sahitya", *Vasudha*, No. 58, July-September, p. 28.
21. Ibid., p. 24.
22. Ibid., p. 38.
23. Sadanand Shahi (2005), "Bhartiya Samaj Mein Dalit Ki Davedari: Premchand Sandarbh", *Vartman Sahitya,* July, 2005, p. 89.
24. Manager Pandey, (2005), "Hindi Curriculum with a Perspective of Dalit Studies", in Arun Kumar and Sanjay Kumar (eds), *Dalit Studies in Higher Education,* Deshkal Publication, Delhi.
25. Subhash Sharma (2009), "Text and Context: A Sociological Analysis of Dalit Character in Hindi Novels", *Hindi*, July-September, 2009.

3

Dalit Saint Poets of Bhakti Movement

Pride and Prejudice

Bhakti (devotion) movement began in South India as early as 8th century CE. However, the idea and action of bhakti movement spread all over India in coming centuries (especially in 14th to 17th century). Interestingly, saint poets from all castes ranging from Brahmins to dalits and even non-Hindus (Muslims) joined it with full enthusiasm. In Tamil, Marathi and Hindi languages and literatures many dalit saint poets composed poems and songs/hymns expressing their joys and sorrows in different ways. Some of them (like Marathi saint poet, Chokhamela and Hindi saint poet, Raidas or Ravidas) expressed their self-experiences in daily life, especially their lower place in a hierarchical stratified society. As Eleanor Zelliot and Rohini Mokashi-Punekar in *Untouchable Saints* (2005) rightly point out, "Although time and the oral tradition have undoubtedly changed their songs, one still has a sense that these are the first authentic voices of untouchables, those outside the fourfold Varna system, and the only voices until the nineteenth century. In the South, there are no such voices. All that has survived from Tiruppan Alvar and Nandanar is one ecstatic song of praise of Vishnu".

Here we take up three dalit saint poets: one each from Tamil, Marathi and Hindi languages/literatures. In Tamil language the oldest dalit saint poet was Tiruppan Alvar (8th century CE). He composed only one poem of eleven verses in praise of Lord Ranganatha (Vishnu) at Srirangam. His poem is being recited both at Srivaishnav temples as well as at homes since the 11th century. His poem represents the typical 'sanatan' Hindu tradition without any protest or questioning the hierarchal social order. Actually, the title 'Alvar' was given by the Srivaishnavas to twelve saint poets, meaning 'who are deeply immersed in the love of Vishnu'. The term 'Tiru' refers to 'Shri' and 'pan' means untouchable. But 'pan' also means music and 'panan' means Tamil minstrel. Unlike other Alvars, Tiruppan does not use his name in the last verse of his poem. The oldest biography of Alvars is found in 'Divya Suri Charitam' in Sanskrit; then 'Guru Parampara Prabhavam' I and II (13th and 15th centuries); Alvarkal Vaibhavam (in Tamil in 15th century) and 'Periya Tirumudi Ataivu' (in Tamil in 16th century). According to all traditional hagiographies (mix of fact and myth), Tiruppan Alvar was an incarnation of Srivatsa (the mole on Vishnu's chest). He was born as Pancham (fifth varna). His divine nature was hidden by the surroundings, it is described, he was given pure food, he never wept, etc. Vasudha Narayanan comments on this aspect: "It is very significant that in all these ways the 'higher' caste authors of these biographies tend to insulate and protect the poet from his untouchable birth. The point is seen to be a divine incarnation, a recipient of Lord Ranganatha's grace, not tainted by impure food or surroundings." By the age of 18, he is said to play the 'veena' sweetly but still would not enter Lord Vishnu's temple, so goddess Lakshmi asks the Lord to bring him to the inner sanctum sanctorum. Lord Vishnu tells the priests that the oldest and highest clan is that of the devotees. But Tiruppan refuses to enter because he considers himself a sinner. Thus, it is noteworthy that the argument shifts from 'lowliness through birth' to 'lowliness due to sin'. Finally, the Lord directs a Brahmin priest, Loka Saranga Muni, to bring Tiruppan. But since he again refuses, the priest along with others forcibly brings him on his shoulders – Tiruppan still not putting his foot on the floor inside the temple and thereby maintains the purity and sanctity of the temple.

In a later hagiography, it is mentioned that Loka Saranga Muni went to river Kaveri to bring water for ritual bath of the deity. There Tiruppan was singing; the priest asked him to move away but Tiruppan was deeply engrossed in singing and did not hear him. Then he threw a stone at Tiruppan whose forehead started bleeding. When Muni reached the temple with a pitcher of water, he found Lord's forehead bleeding. Lord's voice told him about his sin and he was directed to bring Tiruppan on his shoulders. But this story is not included in old hagiographies, hence it is an interpolation in modern versions 'when prejudices were even stronger'. Now, the question arises who inserted this. Since such hagiographies were traditionally with Brahmins, they seem to have interpolated it "to convince the non-Shrivaishnava Brahmins that Loka Saranga Muni did after all have a 'politically correct' attitude towards the 'Untouchables' at least unless commanded otherwise by the Lord" (Vasudha Narayanan). Further, *Amar Chitra Katha* (a Hindi comic book) tells that Tiruppan was abandoned by his parents and was brought up by the sweepers but panans are described as singers in early Tamil literature. Hence, this distortion is probably due to north Indian stereotype. Further, this comic mentions that when Tiruppan was allowed by the Brahmin priests to enter the temple, he was full of anger and sorrow: "The priests have made my Lords a prisoner, he cannot see those whom he wants to see". Further, he utters, "I wish I were dead, Lord! With death the questions of birth and impurity cease to exist. No one can separate us then". Furthermore, it portrays senseless violence heaped on Tiruppan. Since these details are not in older versions, these are interpolations. The agenda of social reform is visible when Amar Chitra Katha mentions: "Even as early as the time of Buddha, Hinduism was already vitiated by the hierarchy of the caste system ... the caste system is still a blot on Hindu society despite the relentless campaigns carried on against it by enlightened social reformers and thinkers through the ages ...."

However, all hagiographies mention that when Tiruppan sang inside the temple, the Lord accepted him with his body and Tiruppan ultimately disappeared into the sacred feet of the Lord. Actually two Alvars, Antal (woman bhakta) and Tiruppan disappeared into the deity. Antal had refused to marry a human being and insisted to get wedded to the Lord as an incarnation of goddess Earth. So Tiruppan was also seen as a unique singer (all singers could not get entry inside the temple). Here the paradigm is a divine being, not a social role model. In his poem, Tiruppan's depiction is a particular and local manifestation identifying with the Vishnu manifestation in the sacred hill of Tirumala Tirupati and with the generic Vishnu of the Puranas.

First verse of his poem shows humility to the Lord:

'Pure Lord
Primordial Lord
Faultless one
Who made me a servant?
of his servants'.

Here 'servant of servants' is Vasudha Narayanan's realistic translation whereas Steven Hopkins translates the phrase as 'slave of slaves' but slavery has absolutely a different connotation in western world. Further, he depicts in the fifth verse:

'Destroying the bonds
of my ancient sins
he made me his own, his love
keeping me so,
the other day
he entered inside me'.

Here the poet Tiruppan admits that Lord had exonerated him of his old sins. He made him his own and he entered inside him – that is, he not only embraced him outwardly but also absorbed him inwardly. In the tenth verse he expresses his desire and inner voice:

'Dark as the stormy cloud
Cowherd whose mouth
Swallowed butter'.

'Lord who captured my heart
King of the sky lords
Lord of the jewel, Arankam
My ambrosia.
My eyes, which have seen him
Cannot see anything else.'

Here, the poet, Tiruppan is of the clear view that he does not want to see worldly things after seeing the Lord closely and inwardly. But, unlike many dalit saint poets of that era, Tiruppan does not mention social status of the untouchable caste. He is spellbound by the Lord's beauty, love, benevolence, powerfulness, purity, faultlessness, righteousness, sacredness, brightness, fragrance and so on. One may be puzzled why an untouchable poet, considered impure and profane, frequently talks if Lord's purity and sacredness. This description, of contrast and assimilation with a Hindu god does not fit in with the current dalit assertion where typical Hindu tradition is questioned and abdicated, rather an alternative Buddhist tradition (of B.R. Ambedkar) is adopted by a substantial section of dalits. But also notable is the fact that during the Bhakti period many dalit poets did not question the Hindu social order and its religious texts, temples and rituals – as did non-dalit poets like Tulsidas, Surdas, Mirabai Dadu, Malukdas, etc. He praises the Lord for destroying the bonds of his 'ancient sins' but these works are generic in nature, not specific about low social status and wickedness. Similarly, he does not wish to serve other devotees, priests and so on – rather he wants a direct relationship with the Lord as well as equality with humans. Needless to mention here that another Alvar of that time Nammalvar prefers the devotees of the Lord as his masters (even if they are untouchables). Further, Tiruppan talks of Lord of Arankam being the same as the Lord in Venkatam. Like other Alvars, he presumes the primacy of Lord Vishnu.

If we analyse the legacy of Srivaishnava community, we find that Tiruppan (and Antal too) was considered exception to normal social system but other untouchables were not allowed temple entry to worship the Lord or Tiruppan (whose idol was installed in temples and worshipped). Srivaishnava scholars like Pillai Lokacharya observes in 'Sri Vachana Bhushanam' that Tiruppan Alvar is higher than other devotees because being the servant (the lowly), his lowliness was 'natural' while other devotees' lowliness is 'assumed'. Similarly, it is said that Antal's love for the Lord was 'natural' because of being a woman whereas men's love was 'assumed'. A myth is prevalent in South India that once, Ramanuja and his disciples were lost in wilderness, and some untouchables gave them shelter and showed the way. Ramanuja called this group 'tiru Kulattar' (clan belonging to goddess Lakshmi). These people, living in Bangalore, are allowed temple entry but they prefer to worship in their community shrines – some kind of assertion and alternative worship. There are twelve shrines (first one built in honour of Tiruppan Alvar) – four for Lord Vishnu and eight for all Alvars. Many followers (ex-untouchables) wear sacred thread, believing that 'Tiruvaymoli', a composition of Nammalvar and the 'Sacred Collection of Four Thousand Verses' are the Tamil Veda. According to Sri Vipranarayana, there is a biological chain of Srivaishnava devotees on the one hand and a direct link to Alvars, on the other. But Srivaishnava devotees, as Vasudha Narayanan observes, have agreed in theory that bhakti (devotion) transcends all religious prescription but is not so in practice.

II

Chokhamala was a 14th century untouchable saint poet in Maharashtra. He belonged to Varkari community that worships Vitthal (Vithoba) at Pandarpur. The pilgrims, while on a foot journey to Pandarpur, sing songs and hymns (*abhangas*). Vitthal is identified by the stories about the saint poets, not by myths and stories about himself. He stands without a terrifying arsenal carried by many armed Hindu deities. He is a 'swarup' (not avatar) of Vishnu, and sometimes identified with the child form of Krishna. As Fred Dallmayr says, the identity of Vitthal contributes to a feeling that it is "intriguingly placed at the crossroads between the manifest and the non-manifest, between revealment and concealment, familiarity and non-familiarity, or in Indian terminology, between 'saguna' and 'nirguna' conceptions". Further, Rohini Mokashi-Punekar is rightly of the view that Chokhamela's life "captures the paradigmatic ambiguity of Hinduism: its liberating intellectual plurality and its equally restricting social construction".

He belonged to Mahars (the lowliest caste) community of untouchables whose identity in Hindu society is shaped through a bunch of negations. Mahars were considered untouchable because they were dragging out carcasses, considered impure and polluting. He was, like other untouchables, denied education, scriptures, use of wells and tanks, entry into the temple; hence these themes became themes of his poetry. Chokha acknowledges Namdev (a lower caste rebel saint poet) as his guru. Chokha's 'samadhi' is located at the foot of stairs to the Vithoba temple (Pandarpur).

As per weaving of one legend and poem, once Chokhamela stood the whole day in front of the temple and at night the priests locked up the main doors of the temple and went away. Thereafter Vithoba himself came out and embraced Chokhamela and led him by hand to the innermost sanctum sanctorum. Vithoba took out his 'tulsi' garland and put it around Chokhamela's neck. So Chokhamela being very pleased lay down on the sands of river Chandrabhaga. On the other hand, the priests found the golden necklace of Vithoba missing. They suspected Chokhamela when they found him wearing the golden necklace while lying on the river's sands. So he was punished by tying him to the bullocks to be dragged; but these bullocks refused to move despite being lashed. Finally, Vithoba revealed the truth. Chokhamela's poem is remarkable:

'They thrash me, Vithu
now don't walk so slow.
the Pandits whip,
some crime,
don't know what:
How did Vithoba's necklace came around your neck?

They curse and strike
and say I polluted you.
Do not send the cur at your door
away,
Giver of everything,
You,
Chakrapani,
Yours is the deed.
With folded hands,
Chokha begs
I revealed your secret,
Don't turn away.'

This poem reveals that Vithoba touches and eats with Chokhamela and gave him the garland – these favours are not done to Brahmin priests. Since then the devotee untouchables of Vithoba wear tulsi beads as a mark of respect to Chokhamela. Even today pilgrims to Pandarpur belonging to all castes recite this *abhanga* but he is not as popular as Namdev or Tukaram (lower caste saint poets) – probably because of his Mahar identity. But the present dalits – Buddhists – have not given Chokhamela a due place because his protest "is contained in bhakti" and also because "he accepts his karma, his birth as an untouchable due to his previous deeds" (Rohini Mokashi-Punekar).

Chokha had died along with other Mahar labourers when part of a wall (they were repairing) collapsed on them. When Namdev went to pick up his remains, he found his bones chanting 'Vitthal'. Hence, his bones were buried at the foot of the stairs of Vithoba temple – where he used to stand all day long in worship. Now all devotees have to visit Chokha's shrine first before entering the main temple. Chokha's poem relates to rural professions of labourers:

'The saviour of his devotees,
who never turns away.
hurries to help them
with their chores
he dusts and cleans
and fetches water,

the upholder of dharma;
saves from the searing
flames of nirvana.
He keeps the cows
at the milkman's house
and happily with others
breaks the pot of curd ...
says Chokha, he is so tender:
his devotees know him
as a fond mother.'

In many abhangs, Vitthal is addressed as mother (mauli). According to A.K. Ramanujan, in bhakti poetry, not only the poet is a woman before god but also god is a loving mother but, as Rohini Mokashi-Punekar says "has little control over the injustices and cruelties of the patriarchal family. Divinity becomes a powerless feminine principle, thus turning the traditional hierarchy topsy-turvy". Further, there is egalitarianism only in theory because, in practice, while going to Pandarpur different castes walk and eat together amongst their own groups. As the sociologist, Irawati Karve rightly observes, the 'dindi' (group) with which she was walking sang Chokha's abhangs but observed all purity rituals of the Brahmins, not eating together with other lower caste members of the dindi. Thus, one may say that this 'varkari' movement could not yield much results, yet this quiet movement has been more flexible and durable. Actually, dalit movement originated and took roots here and its oral tradition contributed to Marathi literature in a dynamic way with irony. For instance, Chokhamela's following abhang is radical:

'The Vedas and the Shastras polluted;
the puranas inauspicious, impure;
the body, the soul contaminated; the manifest
Being is the same.
Brahma polluted, Vishnu too;
Shankar is impure, inauspicious.
birth impure, dying is impure
says Chokha,

pollution stretches
without beginning
and end.'

Similarly, in another abhang, Chokhamela recites and questions the very conception of impurity, untouchability and thus the caste system based on it:

'Five elements compound the impure body;
all things mix,
thrive in the world.
Then who is pure and who impure?
The body is rooted in impurity.
From the beginning to the end,
endless impurities
heap themselves.
Who is it can be made pure?
Says Chokha,
I am struck with wonder.
Can there be any such
beyond pollution?'

But in the following abhang, Chokhamela accepts the 'karma' theory of Hindu religion (destiny guided by actions in previous birth) which is rejected by present-day dalit writers, intellectuals and social reformers:

'I will give you a key:
what must be, will be;
what will not, cannot.
All joy and sorrow you will see
are based in karma.
Don't fret Chokha, says God,
this is my promise:
you are the best of devotees.'

Thus, about 400 abhangas (of Chokhamela and his family – wife, sister, sister's husband, and son) have spiritual impulse first and literary creations only later. Chokha's voice has a combination of both spiritual aspirations and physical deprivations. Since abhangas are oral in nature, there is no final version (like Kabir's Sakhis, Sabads and Ramainis). Chokhamela's wife Soyrabai, their son Karmamela, his sister Nirmala and her husband Banka composed abhangas. To know the importance of Chokhamela, one needs to see his impact on later generations of untouchables, especially Mahars. When B.R. Ambedkar openly favoured conversion of Mahars in 1935, Kisan Fago Bansode (1879–1946) opposed him. He named one of his newspapers, *Chokhamela* and urged protest through the following poem:

> 'Why do you endure curses?
> Chokha went into the temple resolutely.
> You are the descendents of Chokha.
> Why do you fear to enter the temple?
> Brace yourself like a wrestler,
> Come, together let us conquer pollution.'

Though B.R. Ambedkar had a different path from Chokhamela, yet he dedicated with honour his book *The Untouchables* to Chokhamela, Nandanar and Ravidas (Raidas). Ambedkar's dissenting view was that the untouchables had been Buddhists, forced into degradation when a Brahminical revival in the 4th century had marginalised that religion. Chokhamela is seen throughout as a Mahar (no myth of being born as a Brahmin as in case of Raidas). Earlier, no Mahar could go beyond the 'samadhi' of Chokhamela but in 1947 a Brahmin Gandhian, Sane Guruji fasted in front of the temple for dalits' entry into the temple and since then temple entry is open to all. Pandarpur pilgrimage is actually more a democratising and humanising tradition than a revolutionary one. We tend to agree with Eleanor Zelliot: "It is difficult to see Chokhamela as a revolutionary figure; it is easy to see him and his family as a proof of two things: first, creativity dwells at all levels; second, the idea of pollution is rejected in no uncertain terms by even the most devout of untouchables".

Chokhamela's tradition is still living and changing. He has been represented in poetry, drama, music and film by contemporary creative persons. Veer Savarkar wrote a musical play 'Sangit Uhshap' (antidote to the curse) by utilising the image and character of Chokhamela to project his views about socio-political reforms. Its first performance was done on 9 April 1927, but on the suggestion of the Censor Board its tragic ending was changed to a happy ending. The anti-Islamic and anti-Christian sentiments were combined with the message of eradication of untouchability; in this play Savarkar draws an affectionate picture of Mahar children by invoking a sense of pride as a Mahar – it is more glorious to love and die as a Hindu than to convert to Christianity or Islam. The greatness of Hinduism is expressed through the character of Chokhamela who hails Hinduism as a superior religion and provider of salvation to the downtrodden. Chokhamela explains to fellow untouchables about cleanliness, devotion and willingness to serve God. He praises Brahminism by telling his son Karmamela: "don't make such unbecoming poisonous remarks against the Brahmin caste. A Brahmin is the third eye of knowledge of Lord Mahadev of our great Hindu Dharma". Further, one female character, a Mahar girl Kamalini, hates her Mahar lover Shankar because he renounces Hinduism in favour of conversion. She claims to be a follower of Chokhamela and for Hindu dharma she is willing to lay down her life. Finally, some opportunistic Brahmins, Kshatriyas and Vaishyas complain to the Muslim king that Chokhamela is corrupting Hindu dharma by trying to enter the temple. Muslim king encourages him to convert to Islam but Chokhamela confirms his loyalty to Hinduism: "Yes, I am a Hindu. I am a Mahar, a sweeper who cleans the traditional circular path around Lord Vitthal's shrine". Thus, Savarkar shows divine justice to be preferred by Chokhamela to social justice (Anil Sapkal).

In another play, 'Yugayatra' (by M.B. Chitnis, an assistant of B.R. Ambedkar) in 1956, the character of Chokhamela is depicted realistically with oppression of the time. He is shown as a bonded labour of the village headman but not allowed to enter Vithoba temple even when standing on its door for long. Then he sends a message to the Lord through Janabai, who is from a lower caste but not an untouchable and is allowed to enter the temple: "My last johar (Mahar greeting) to God. Tell him that this devoted servant remained loyal to him till the end". There Chokhamela accepts the destined karma theory by even quoting Sant Gyaneshwar. But Chokhamela is casteless, representing the huge oppressed masses and he emerges to see the Lord but he is aware of casteism. He says that the life of the untouchables has become a defilement embodied throughout. The play depicts the exploitation of Chokhamela at the hands of 'deshpandes' and 'patils' (upper caste village officials). It also shows that he was crushed under a wall while working. Thus, Chitins has realistically depicted the deep devotion of Chokhamela, on the one hand, and the hypocrisy of the upper castes towards him, on the other (Anil Sapkal).

A Marathi film 'Sant Chokhamela' was directed by D.K. Kale in 1941 showing him working dutifully as a Mahar but engrossed in devotion to Vitthal. Once his shadow falls on a Brahmin, Bindu Madhav who treats this as an act of defilement, hence denies him entry into the street leading to Pandarpur temple. But he continues his prayer. Consequently, Bindu Madhav's son, Anant Bhatt becomes Chokhamela's follower. Chokhamela stops Mahar tradition of sacrificing a male buffalo before the deity Mariai. But Mahars regard this as a blow to their pride. They along with the upper castes oppose Chokhamela but Vithal helps him by appearing as a Mahar to share his meal. Thus, while underlining the caste conflict, this film highlights the story of Anant Bhatt in a progressive way. In the end, the bones of Chokhamela repeat the names of Vithoba, and Namdev declares that Chokha has become God incarnate. In the film the character of Chokhamela says, "What kind of a Brahmin is he if he has no mercy, no compassion". He feels the pain of Mahar caste but accepts the theory of Karma, "It is our credo, our duty to serve. The son serves his parents, the breadwinner serves his family, and the lowest of society serves the Brahmin. One community serves the other. I serve you, you serve me – This is the basis of the credo of service" (Anil Sapkal).

Another Marathi film, 'Johar Maybap' (1950) was directed by Ram Gabale and famous Marathi writer P.L. Deshpande played the role of Chokhamela, and Sulochana acted the role of his wife Soyrabai. Its story was written by the

Venkatesh Madgulkar, and screenplay, dialogue and verses by G.D. Madgulkar. Poverty as well as affection in the family are vividly depicted. Vithoba's early appearance before Chokhamela reflects a sign of approval of his devotion. Chokhamela is shown as a bonded labour of the village headman doing all odd jobs, Though in poems, Banka accepts Chokhamela as his guru but in the film Banka introduces him to 'bhagvat dharma'. Though evils of caste system are shown in the film, yet poverty is shown as the major cause of all troubles. Instead of inhuman caste system, a liberal social situation is shown. Namdev declares to Chokhamela, "All of you are Vitthal". Chokhamela is a virtuous and moral person but is opposed by the village headman. However, the priest Anant Bhatt is close to him. The character of Bindu Madhav is absent. Rather, Chokhamela is shown accompanying Anant's mother to Pandarpur. Chokhamela was engrossed in devotion when the village headman drags him away to construct the boundary wall around Manglevedhe. But the wall collapses and he dies. Vithoba directs Namdev to bring his bones to place in 'samadhi', to be constructed in front of his temple. Here is the effective use of music and moving performances about devotion. However, casteist humiliation is missing in the film. (Anil Sapkal). Thus, a comparative analysis of two plays and two films shows that Chokhamela's devotion to Vithoba is well represented but other aspects of his life and perspective were depicted with specific ideology or movement or partial understanding of his persona.

III

Raidas (Ravidas) or Rohidas (in Maharashtra) was a dalit saint poet born in Varanasi. His caste of tanners (charmakar) was considered physically and socially impure because in their occupation dead animals were carried outside the village and were deskinned, and finally they made leather shoes. Further, because of Karma theory it was believed that people were destined by actions of the previous birth. There are six sources of Raidas, coloured by their writers' religious, social, economic and ideological views. The first source is Nabhadas's 'Bhaktamal' (garland of devotees), written at the turn of 17th century (1600 AD). There it is described that the 'banis' (verses) of Raidas were skilled in the knots (granthis) of doubt, but were not opposed to the Vedas, Shastras, and the practice of good people – that is, he did not rebel against Hindu order. Further, through God's grace, Raidas attained the ultimate goal in this body. Finally, he showed pride in his lineage, caste and ashram – i.e., he was not ashamed of his birth. But Nabhadas's description lacks specific concrete details.

Second portrayal by Anantdas in 'Raidas Parichai' (1588 but unpublished) is full of magic and miracles to prove that Raidas was a great saint. He declares that Ravidas was a Brahmin in previous birth but he ate meat and kept an untouchable co-wife. Further, his parents in present birth were irreligious; Raidas did not suckle mother's milk for four days. Then Ramanand, directed by heavenly voice, appears and initiates his entire family, only then Rabidas suckles. His parents don't share his devotion and he is deprived of his share of property. Raidas's devotion makes him a saint despite his lowest social standing (James G. Lotchtefeld).

In the third portrayal by Priyadas in 'Bhaktirasabodhini' – a commentary on 'Bhaktamal' – in 1712 shows that birth in a Charmakar caste is not the result of Raidas' previous birth's actions (karma) but because of a curse in previous birth. Then he was a Brahmin and disciple of Ramananda, and he served food to his guru by begging from some specific families. But one day due to a storm he did not move out and accepted food from a merchant who did business with Charmakars. Knowing this, Ramanand cursed him to be born as a Charmakar. Thus, Priyadas's account reinforces the conventional view that Charmakars are polluting and lowliest – even doing business with dalits is considered impure. Further, as per Priyadas, Raidas did not suckle his 'untouchable' mother's milk due to her touch. Again, Raidas is saved by Ramanand who initiates Raidas alone. Since initiation is considered as 'second birth', and one's guru a parent, Ramanand becomes Raidas's real father – thus, although Raidas is born in a lowly family he does not belong to it in reality. In addition, Raidas is kicked out by his father.

If we compare the accounts of Anantdas and Priyadas, following points emerge (Lochtefeld) : first, regarding Raidas's birth, Priyadas shows greater ambivalence than Anantdas – for the latter, Ramanand's appearance is merely dramatic, for Priyadas it is continuation of an established guru-disciple bond, confirming that Raidas is not a Charmakar. Second, as per Anantdas, Ramanand initiated the entire family of Raidas – availability of devotion to all – but Priyadas uses initiation for only Raidas as a way to remove the stigma of being a charmakar. Third, both writers mention that Raidas was treated badly by his family, Anantdas's account reflects their individual shortcomings but Priyadas tries to establish that Raidas never really belonged to them. Fourth, both writers show him as a saint. Both writers show that Raidas did not suckle for four days, but Priyadas adds that Raidas regretted for his error and refused to suckle until initiated by Ramanand – hence Raidas was not an ordinary child. Fifth, both writers describe tales in which Raidas displays superhuman powers, e.g., Raidas goes to his disciple Jhali, queen of Chittore but Brahmins refuse to take food with Raidas who goes to a corner but all Brahmins see the figure of Raidas in between them and later Raidas peals his skin to reveal a golden sacred thread! This established his devotion, sacredness and Brahminhood. Sixth, both writers show him to worship with an image (Anantdas explicitly describes him a 'saguna', devotee) but Raidas actually worshipped (and also in poems) 'nirguna' (formless) god. Seventh, Anantdas shows the tension between dharma and bhakti, between a hierarchical social system and essentially egalitarian religious practice. He tries to subvert the social system completely but Priyadas tries to rehabilitate Raidas as an individual, leaving the social system intact. Though both accounts are hagiographic but while Priyadas' ambivalence is about Raidas being both a saint and Charmakar, Anatdas focuses on devotion.

Fourth portrayal of Raidas by Chandrika Prasad Jigyasu in his 'Sant Pravar Raidas Sahib' (1956) is deliberately "A Discriminating Biography: Written from a Buddhist point of view" (as subtitle says). According to its author, Raidas was a Buddhist, drawn into the Hindu tradition later. He mentions B.R. Ambedkar as an example of the fact that great spiritual leaders can come from any community. He appeals to all to accept Buddhism and abdicate Hinduism as 'urine and faeces'. In 1956, Ambedkar had converted to Buddhism. Rejecting Priyadas's account that Raidas was a Brahmin in previous birth, criticizing birth due to curse, not suckling for four days and surviving, he emphasises that Raidas was a Charmakar and never claimed to be anything else. Brahmins cannot accept that low caste people can come to know God by themselves. He gives an account of Raidas's birth: One day Raidas's father was passing through the deer park at Sarnath where Buddha first preached. An ascetic there was very fond of 'khir' (pudding), so Ravidas's parents supplied it, consequent to which the ascetic promised them a son. Jigyasu claims that an old sadhu at Varanasi had told him this – but this is equally irrational and unscientific. Second, criticising Priyadas he further says that Raidas never mentioned in his poems that he was a disciple of Ramanand. Third, disagreeing with Nabhadas, he argues that Raidas' poetry was distant from Hindu tradition. But, surprisingly, he uses many mystical stories and miracles from Bhaktamal to buttress his point that Raidas was a great saint, though in his book, Jigyasu keeps one chapter on 'Buddhists are not convinced by miracles'! To him, miracles were harsh tests of his devotion. This contradiction is duly pointed out by James G. Lochtefeld, "On the one hand Jigyasu shows the rationality and rejection of the miraculous characterising in both early Buddhism and twentieth century scientific thought. But, on the other hand, he also fixes a full account of these miracles, as if these could provide further proof of Ravidas's sanctity. It seems as if Jigyasu wants to simultaneously deny and affirm these miracles".

Fifth portrayal of Raidas is in *Amar Chitrakatha* (1988). There it is mentioned that real problem is not poverty but lower status associated with tanning. Raidas's teacher, Sandan Swami tells him that distinction between pure and impure occupations are the product of ignorant persons.

Later, Raidas tells his followers: "Do not be ashamed of yourself. Do not be afraid of your caste. Do your work with dignity and bow before no one but God". This book shows that parents of Raidas were taking bath in Ganga and came daily for a 'holy dip'. They pray to the sun god for a son. As per teachings of Sandan Swami he breaks his mental block – stops thinking himself as a Charmakar and then destroys the distinction between 'self' and 'other'. He sees God everywhere and says that seeing God only in an image puts the image between oneself and God. To name is to limit and particularise but God transcends human conceptual capacities. Hence, Raidas says, he refers to God solely as a 'name'. Later, in the story, Mirabai visits Raidas and says that she cannot bear to be separated from Lord Krishna. In response, Raidas says that since she is already with God, how could there be any separation? Mira, finally, sets the image down, feeling liberated from slavery to a statue. Further the conflict between Raidas and his parents arise due to his compassion for the poor for whom he steals shoes and money from his parents.

Sixth portrayal of Ravidas (Raidas) comes from his 39 poems included in Adi Granth (1604) and 8 poems in Fatehpur Manuscript (1582). These poems are benchmarks defining the real Raidas. These poems, however, depict his religious concerns, mentioning little about his personal life. In one poem the image of absolute identity with God is depicted:

'What is the difference
Between you and me
Me and you?
Like the gold and the bracelet
Water and waves.'

In another poem the identification is less direct, phrased in terms of associated things:

'If you are the mountain,
I am the peacock;

If you are the moon,
I am the Chakora bird.'

Third poem shows a humble man with little faith in his capacities; his only hope lies in surrender to God:

'Tanner Ravidas says:
My birth is low
My people are low
My caste is also low
Raja Ramachandra
I have come to you for refuge!'

However, in one poem, he talks of 'begampur' (the sorrowless city) where there is no anxiety, no jealousy, no taxes or trade; there is 'no second or third' (social hierarchy) – all are equal. People live there comfortably – this is a utopian version indicating that his society was wanting. However, he seems less interested in changing the society than in transcending it altogether. In one poem, he compares himself to a fish that never forgets her home, even after her body has been cut up for cooking, every piece still longs for water. This conveys a sense of alienation and displacement. Though he does not mention his guru's name, Raidas recognises his significance: through guru's grace one attains God and does not go to hell; through true guru (sadguru) one can know the saints; he exhorts people to follow guru's path. Often 'sadguru' is another way of referring to the Divine. He does not favour rituals:

> 'One cleans the outside body with water, but inside there are various faults. How can one become pure, this is like the elephant's bath.'

In another poem he tells that a man of good family performing rituals without devotion is no better than an untouchable. Though he does not reject Vedas and Shastras, (as Jigyasu thought) in one poem he says: "O Lord, the Vedas call you the Inner Knower, but they do not know your glory" – thus he is not totally unopposed to Vedas (as Nabhadas asserted). Thus, he has some kind of ambivalence regarding Vedas.

Thus, against these six portrayals, his poems express authenticity. One poem of his talks about devotion as the ultimate decider:

> 'In whatever family a good vaishnav is found,
> Whether they be high caste or outcaste lord or pauper,
> the world will know the one by his flawless fragrance.
> Whether one's heart is Brahmin or Vaishya,
> Shudra or Kshatriya,
> Dom, Chandal, or Mlechcha,
> through the worship of the Lord, one becomes pure, and
> liberates the self and both family lines.'

In another poem he questions the very conception of impurity:

> 'The baby calf makes the cow's udder unclean,
> the bee spoils the flower and the fish, the sea.
> Oh mother! What can I bring to offer in worship to Govind.
> There is no perfect flower to be found!
> The snake has spoiled the sandalwood tree;
> the poison and the nectar are one.
> Incense, lamps, offerings of food, fragrances:
> How can I, your servant, offer these?
> I would offer my body, my mind;
> through the grace of guru I will find the one without stain.
> I cannot worship you and offer rituals,
> So, Ravidas says: What is to be my end?

He declares his tanner caste but tells that devotion to God has brought upper castes to bow down to him:

> Oh people of the city!
> My notorious caste is Chamar!
> In my heart is the essence of all good qualities, Ram – Govinda
> My caste is Kutabadhala. I carry cattlehides
> All around Benares always.
> Now the Brahmins and leaders bow down before me.
> Ravidas, your servant, has taken the refuge of your name.

In another poem he calls himself 'the servant of servants'. It is noteworthy that Sikh's Guru Granth Sahib consists of forty-one poems of Raidas – here "a dalit forms part of the spirituality of a major religion", says Chandrabhan Prasad, a dalit scholar who quotes Engels: "Every struggle against feudalism at the time had to take on a religious disguise", and Ravidas did that centuries back. Actually, Raidas has got a large number of followers called 'Raidasis' or Ravidasis.' Raidasi Sikh migrants in US and Europe have built temples and gurudwaras in his name and celebrate continuously by organising seminars, discourses and festivals. His followers made the first Raidas temple in Varanasi. But like Kabirpanthis, Raidasis, too, have indulged in rituals (instead of devotion) and different sub-sects, groups or individuals indulge in fighting for the capture and control of the seat of power there.

From the above, following critical points emerge about dalit saint poets in different parts of India during Bhakti movement:

First, the voices of dalit saint poets are the first authentic voices of the untouchable communities.

Second, these saint poets opened their following to all humans, irrespective of barriers like caste and creed, language and residence. A sense of companionship and brotherhood exists in their poems.

Third, all saint poets praise and worship God as 'saguna' (with qualities) or 'nirguna' (the formless) and see in them the saviours of the oppression, untouchability and helplessness.

Fourth, all dalit saint poets are conscious of their lowest caste position in a hierarchical social system. They dislike and humbly protest against the caste, impurity and pollution but they did not rebel against the existing stratified social systems as such. They often see individual liberation through devotion to God, but not radical collective liberation from the socio-economic, political and religious inequalities. Contemporary dalit writers criticise them for being liberal and not questioning the caste system itself.

Fifth, they are proximately associated with various myths, legends and anecdotal tales reflecting unrealistic magic and miracles to establish their authority of great sainthood. Contemporary dalit writers usually question the Hindu religion and social order on the ground that it has various miracles which are not rational and scientific in everyday life, but they deliberately ignore the similar magic and miracles associated with dalit saint poets.

Sixth, these dalit saint poets often developed new sects like Ravidasis (like Kabirpanthis and Dadupanthis), or annual Pandarpur pilgrimage or new temples (Raidas temple in Varanasi, Punjab, US, etc.) or 'samadhis' at the foot of the stairs of ancient temples (Chokhamela) – reflecting some kind of latent and partial inclusion in the Hindu social-religious order.

Seventh, these dalit saint poets used vernacular languages of the masses for mass appeal through their poems, songs and hymns. This process of democratisation of regional literature is noteworthy since medieval period in different parts of India. Their personal self-experiences with caste-linked occupations popularised new terms, idioms, tools and techniques of depiction, and metaphors from grassroots reality.

Finally, a new trend of establishing personal bonds with the divine power without any mediators (like priests) opened new vistas of word and deed. What feminists adopted in the second half of the 20th century for ventilation of their grievances under the idiom of 'personal is political', was expressed many centuries back by dalit saint poets, though in a latent form that may be accurately called 'personal is social' because liberation from the caste prejudices could be achieved through devotion to God and the so-called upper castes also became their followers and disciples in due course of time.

Thus, the poems and songs as well as the religious discourses of dalit saint-poets did bring functional and incremental (not fundamental) changes in socio-religious and cultural order of Hindu society in India during Bhakti movement period (14th to 17th century) in more than one way.

4

Theories of Sociology of Literature

A Critique

Sociological study of literature began in the nineteenth century in the Western countries. In the last century, it developed with much rigour and sophistication. Attempts made so far by different sociologists and social critics to analyse the links/conjunctions of literature and society are of varying nature. There are some scholars who follow deterministic approach and consider social and historical conditioning of literary works to be the valid way of understanding them. There are some other intellectuals for whom literature is a force, being ahead of time, indicating new ideas and paths of progress. Besides these, one finds quite a few more approaches adopted for the study of literature. Thus, there are various views of sociology of literature.[1] Following major perspectives/theories of sociology of literature are discussed:

(a) Realism.
(b) Socialist realism.
(c) Marxist theory.
(d) Critical realism.
(e) Postmodernism.

Realism

H.A. Taine (1823–93) of France is recognised as the father of sociology of literature. Under the rubric of realism, first stream was positivism. Madame de Stael (1766–1817), in a nascent form, and later Taine, in a more systematic way, pioneered a positivist theory of sociology of literature. They tried to develop a rigorous method for analysing the literary work in order to develop a science of literature that would point out the causes of appearance of a particular writer or his literary creation. They considered literature as an 'external' fact. Stael argued that literature is influenced by law, morality and religion and, in turn, influences them. Further, the natural environment and race also influence the nature and style of literature. She also added that the novel's development depended on the rise of a strong middle class (as this class encourages necessary conditions of art like liberty and sincerity) and its close association with the respectful position of women in society, as in 19th century Britain. To her, the novel is a new form of art in modern era.[2] For Taine, a literary work reflected the society at large, its environment and racial forces, therefore it may be seen as a 'document' of its period. He contends that the novel is a "portable mirror which can be conveyed everywhere and is most convenient for reflecting all aspects of life and nature".[3] In Taine's view, novel depicts what is existing at a particular time. It is merely an accumulation of social facts that can be scientifically analysed. Scientific method neither praises anything nor condemns it, rather it simply yields the salient features. To him, a literary creation is not merely a record of the imaginary flights of a particular person, rather it is a product of his/her rewriting of the contemporary customs as well as an expression of a special kind of mentality. In his works *History of English Literature* and *Philosophy of Art*, he makes out four major premises: (a) First, literature has social bases, hence it is a social product. Race (genetic features, mental make-up, and physical structure), environment (natural and social) and epoch (main ideas of an epoch make an ideological frame which influences the thinking of the whole society) constitute the social bases. (b) Second, the significance of author. The goal of the entire literary exercise, according to him, is to know man and an artist explores the truth of life in his society and epoch, hence he has a special position. (c) Third, literature is the mirror of society. However, such literature can be produced only by great artists. Artistic greatness enhances the value which qualifies to be a social document or evidence. (d) Finally, the readers have a role in the construction and change of the forms of literature; the responses of readers influence the selection of a subject, content and form.[4]

To such positivists, the function of a novel remained more or less confined to transmission of social information to the readers. The positivistic sociology of literature was basically deterministic in that it presented a mechanical, simplified, one-to-one or causal relationship between the society and literature ignoring other aspects such as the literary consciousness and imaginative power of the writer and his or her complex relationship with social networks.

Thus, realism of 19th century emphasised on the contemporary society, on the one hand, and attempted to use the rigour of natural science in sociology of literature, on the other. Therefore, it may be criticised as literature cannot be as rigorously tested as natural objects.

Socialist Realism

Before discussing about socialist realism, let us briefly discuss about Russian formalism. Russian formalists were interested more in the method or scientific ways of theory of literature, rather than social aspects of literature. Literature was considered as a special use of language. They were concerned with explaining how aesthetic effects are produced by literary devices and how 'literary' is distinct from 'extra-literary'. Actually, in Russia, Moscow Linguistic Circle was founded in 1915. The Society for the Study of Poetic Knowledge was started in Opojaz in 1916. Roman Jakobson was one of the leading figures of the first group and later he founded Prague Linguistic Circle in 1926. Viktor Shklovsky and Boris Elkenbaum were main figures in the second group. The Russian formalists focused on author's technical progress and craft skill. Shklovsky defined literature as "the sum total of all stylistic devices employed in it".[5] Another stream – stucturalist type of formalism – was developed by Roman Jakobson, Tynyanov and Rene Wellek.[6] Later, Mikhail Bakhtin synthesised Russian formalism and Marxism. He and his colleagues, Pavel Medvedev and Valentin Voloshinov, were of the view that despite a consent for linguistic structure of a literary work (as formalists emphasised), language cannot be separated from ideology. Instead of abstract linguistics, they emphasised on language or discourse as a social phenomenon, that is, different manners for different classes in different social and historical situations were duly considered. Bakhtin criticised those linguists like Saussure who considered language as a dead, neutral and static object of investigation. He also rejected the view of the isolated, finished, manologic utterance, divorced from its verbal and actual context. He was also of the view that verbal signs are the area of continuous class struggle because the dominant ruling class will attempt to narrow the meaning of words and make social signs 'uni-accentual' instead of the multi-accentuality. Despite this progressive view, however, he did not consider literature as a direct 'reflection' of social forces, rather he still held the formalistic concern for literary structure. Actually he focused not on the way text reflects society or class interest but the way language is made to derive authority and liberate alternative voices.[7]

Unfortunately, George Plekhanov took a mechanical Marxist position and observed that a sociological analysis consisted of a search for 'sociological equivalents' within literary works, relating literary structures to class structures directly. In his view, cultural history is "a reflection of its classes, of their struggle, one with another".[8] Orthodox socialist realism was the official Communist Party's artistic method in Eastern Europe. It regarded the revolutionary changes in European art, music and literature around 1910 (Picasso, Stravinsky, Schoenberg and T.S. Eliot) as the decadent products of late capitalism. Three principles of Soviet socialist realism are noteworthy:[9] (a) 'Partinost' (commitment to the working class as the cause of the party); (b) 'Narodnost' (popularity) – expressing a high level of social awareness revealing assurance of the true social conditions and feelings of a particular epoch – it is central to both aesthetics and politics;

and (c) Klassovost (class nature of art). Though some of them emphasised only on the commitment of the writer, others treated the class nature of art as a simple matter of writer's explicit class allegiance. Thus, the Soviet socialist realism developed a crude and mechanical Marxist theory of sociology of literature. Williams (1975: 302) also traces out the Soviet socialist realism that had four major elements:

(a) Narodnost – requirement of popular simplicity and traditional clarity – restatement of ordinary technical meaning, in contrast with the difficulties of formalism;
(b) Ideinost – ideological content/attitude;
(c) Partinost – party affiliation – revolutionary, party attitude; and
(d) Tipichnost – typical characters in typical situations, as Engels defined, but it is not something frequently encountered – rather the truly typical is based on 'comprehension of the laws and perspectives of future social development'.

The concept of 'tipichnost' changes 'realism' from its sense of the direct reproduction of observed reality to a 'principled and organised selection'. But is the 'typical' simply "the most deeply characteristic human experience"? Williams says no, because such 'convincingly real' criterion is prevalent in the West in both realist and non-realist art works in technique.

Marxist Theory

Karl Marx had not propounded any specific theory of sociology of literature systematically but he had written about relationship between class consciousness and social existence. Unlike positivists, he gave due importance to consciousness and human activity in producing his or her world. For instance, he wrote, "at the end of every labour process, we get a result that already existed in the imagination of the labourer at its commencement".[10] Marx had taken a dialectical materialistic position about the internal and external world. On the one hand, he realised the dynamic role played by the socio-economic, political and historical conditions for bringing the human consciousness but, on the other hand, he also viewed that man changes his own nature. Thus, man is guided by history as much as he makes the history. This is Marx's concept of 'praxis'; Marx commented on Diderot's novel *Rameau's Nephew* and pointed out that there is no mechanical relationship between artistic creation and economic structure. He introduced the concept of alienation, which is a result of exploitative capitalistic system in which one's sense of wholeness, one's potential many-sidedness including creativity is reduced to a mere fragment, that is, a specialised activity, That is to say that in a capitalist system of production, man becomes a thing and his labour becomes simply a commodity which is used by the capitalist or the state and its organs. Therefore, a creative writer's situation in such a society turns into a struggle against alienation. Thus, he creates his own social world as creativity is the antithesis of alienation. To the question whether literature is simply a reflection of society, Marx replies in negative because between literature and society there is a complex structure of social mediations. Marx has written that the mode of production determines the social, political and economic culture of life-process in general: "it is not the consciousness of man that determines their being but on the contrary their social being that determines their consciousness."[11] However, Alan Swingewood makes two important points as far as Marx's theory of sociology of literature is concerned:[12] first, Marx saw those writers who directly expressed a class interest in their creative works as mediocre artists, for the immediate transposition of economic and political interest into literature transforms it into ideology and thus a bad art; second, in Marx's view, it is only when the writer transcends his own class viewpoint that he reflects truthfully the nature of society and man's relation within it, that is to say, that the creative writer becomes a critique of society, especially because of the dialectical relationship of the artistic activity to social values, individuals, institutions and society at large.

There are many Marxists who have taken divergent positions as far as sociology of literature is concerned. Amongst them Georg Lukacs, Bertolt Brecht, Terry Eagleton, Raymond Williams, Lucien Goldmann, Louis Althusser, A. Gramsci and Fredric Jameson are major critics. Therefore, it becomes imperative to discuss their theoretical views of sociology of literature, especially with reference to novels.

Lukacs, in his works like *History and Class Consciousness* (1923), *The Theory of Novel* (1916), and *Studies in European Realism* (1950), developed 'Hegelian' dialectics and used the concept of reflection. He rejected naturalism of the then European novel and argued that the novel reflects social reality, not by rendering its mere surface appearance but by giving us a "truer, more complete, more vivid and more dynamic reflection of reality".[13] Thus, to Lukacs, to reflect, is 'to frame a mental structure' transposed into words and this reflection is concrete. For instance, a novel may lead a reader 'towards a more concrete insight into reality' going beyond the commonsense understanding of social reality. But he also emphasised there, that a literary work reflects not individual phenomena in isolation but 'the full process of life'. Yet the readers are aware that a literary work is not the reality itself but a 'special form of reflecting reality'. He rejects 'photographic' representation of reality because a true realistic literary work gives us a sense of 'artistic necessity' of the images presented from the complex social life. He pointed out further that modernist writers (Kafka, Beckett, Faulkner) failed to see human existence as a part of a dynamic historical environment. Therefore, they were concerned with formal experiment – with montage, inner monologues, the technique of the 'stream of consciousness', the use of reportage, diaries, etc., and this was a narrow concern for subjective impressions which emerged from advanced individualism of late capitalism. Therefore, they did not have objective realism rather only one dimension of the complex reality. However, when Lukacs was arrested and put into a jail by the government, he realised the realism depicted in Kafka's novels. Secondly, to Lukacs, the novel constitutes an attempt by the modern man to reconcile life (existence) with true self (his essence) through epic narration. Epic is an 'extensive totality', a closed art form in which the hero is never an individual because the epic must describe community's destiny, not individual's. Epic's hero never questions the values of the community and is never lonely. On the contrary, Lukacs points out, the hero (problematical) of the novel is the product of man's alienation from the social world where values are no longer universally binding and individual is not bound to a closed community. So, unlike the epic, novel's hero seeks meaning to his life through individual action; therefore, to Lukacs, novel is an unfinished art-form continuously fluctuating between 'being' and 'becoming' and the novelist tries to impose a sense of wholeness on the fragmented world. Since, in his view, novel seeks to "uncover and construct the concealed totality of life", its hero must seek the meaning of life within a mundane world that denies and frustrates him. Thus, novel comes out of the tension between the 'problematical hero' and the contingent world, the conflict between the universal values (sought by the hero) and the impossibility to realise these in mundane world. Thus, for Lukacs, novel is the antagonism between the external social world (a stranger to ideals and an enemy of interiority) and man's inner soul: "The novel tells of the adventure of interiority, the content of the novel is the story of the soul that goes to find itself, that seeks adventures in order to be proved and tested by them and, by proving itself, to find its own essence."[14]

Thirdly, Lukacs points out that the writer does not transpose a worldview of a class on a literary level, rather reflects in his creation 'the progressive' forces of work in the economic system. But, unlike Taine, he argues that great literature mirrors its age through artist's active participation in 'progressive' social trends. The way a novel mirrors a society is not direct but intentional, because objective reflection depends on writer's attitude towards social development. His depiction of the social world would be objective if he makes a right choice that will be possible in two ways:[15]

(a) If the writer lives in a society with 'progressive' social tendencies such as economically expanding bourgeois class engaged in developing capitalism (e.g., Goethe, Balzac, Stendhal, Tolstoy); or

(b) Living in a politically reactionary period when the bourgeois class has become parasitic and a fetter on the further development of society (in Western Europe post-1848), he struggles against the decadence (e.g., Keller, Mann).

However, Lukacs has been criticised for being remote from reality and close to idealism as Brecht says: "It is the element of capitulation of withdrawal, of utopian idealism which still lurks in Lukacs' essays and which he will undoubtedly overcome, that makes his work, which otherwise contains so much of value, unsatisfactory; for it gives the impression that what concerns him is enjoyment rather than struggle, a way of escape rather than an advance."[16]

Secondly, Lukacs' concentration on Balzac and Goethe is obsolete as he prefers pure or formalistic literary rules for class interest. His attempt to put Tolstoy, Turgnev and Dostoevsky in the generic category of realists is not acceptable due to irrational elements in Dostoevsky. Again, despite Stendhal's 'romanticism' and Balzac's 'fantastic' elements, he puts both of them in the category of realists.

Thirdly, Lukacs considers criticism as a science, not an art, hence the demerits of positivism creep in his theory. Therefore, at times he becomes insensible to the great musicians of language, and his 'method' is unable to explain the complex dialectical relations between literature and society – thus the meditations are ignored and deterministic connections are established.

Finally, Lukacs was also criticised by the scholars of Frankfurt School like Theodor Adorno and Max Horkheimer because Lukacs had declared modernist experimental writers as 'decadent' examples of exclusive concern with the subjectivity of the alienated individual in the fragmented world. Whereas Adorno and Horkheimer appreciated modernist writers like James Joyce, Marcel Proust and Samuel Beckett whose experiments established a distance and effected a detachment that served as an implicit critique of the dehumanising institutions and process of society under capitalism.[17]

Another Marxist critic Brecht is of the view that the illusion of reality should be deliberately shattered by the use of an episodic plot, by protagonists who do not attract the audience's sympathy, by emphasising theatricality in stage and acting, and by other ways of bearing the device of drama so as to produce 'estrangement effects' that will jar audiences out of their passive acceptance of modern capitalist society as a natural way of life, into an attitude not only (as in Adorno) of critical understanding of capitalist shortcomings but of an active engagement with the forces of change.[18] Brecht was of the view that against the increasing barbarism there is only one ally that is the people, who are the victims of barbarism at the most, therefore the authors should turn to the people and 'speak their language'. Thus, for Brecht, 'popular art' and 'realism' are natural allies. Therefore, in order to get a genuine image of life from literature, it should be made comprehensible and profitable to the people, that is, popular. Brecht points out that "the prevailing aesthetic, the price of books and the police have always ensured that there is a considerable distance between the writer and people. Nevertheless, it would be wrong, that is to say, unrealistic, to view the widening of this distance as a purely external one. Undoubtedly special efforts have to be made today in order to be able to write in a popular style".[19] Brecht's concept of popular reference to "a people who not only play a full part in historical development but actively usurp it, force its pace, determine its direction. We have a people in mind that make history, change the world and themselves. We have in mind a fighting people and, therefore, an aggressive concept of what is popular".[20] Thus, for him, popular art is for the masses who are oppressed by the few and who were the 'object of politics' earlier, must now become the 'subject of politics'. But literary works cannot be seen as factories. His concept of realism is "wide and political, sovereign over all conventions".[21] His realism is to discover five things:

(a) 'causal complexes of society';
(b) treating the prevailing view of things as that of 'those in power';
(c) writing from the viewpoint of the class offering broadest solutions;
(d) emphasising the elements of development; and
(e) making possible the concrete and making possible abstraction from it.

But these are 'vast precepts' (that may be extended), and the artist is to use his fantasy, originality, humour and invention in following them. In his words, "we shall not bind, the artist to too rigidly defined modes of narrative".[22] He clarifies that a sensuously written work may not be realistic and a realistic work may not be written in a sensuous style. The question is whether one develops a plot best to reveal the spiritual life of the characters. Therefore, he specifically mentions that to follow the realistic forms of Balzac and Tolstoy means not being realistic because realism is not a simple question of form. Therefore, Brecht demands 'invention' from every writer by going into the depth of complex social reality, because "the truth can be suppressed in many ways and must be expressed in many ways".[23] The suppression of truth is due to different kinds of oppression in different historical periods. To quote him again, "The oppressors do not work in the same way in every epoch. They cannot be defined in the same fashion at all times. There are so many means for them to avoid being spotted. They call their military roads, motorways; their tanks are painted so that they look like MacDuff's woods. Their agents show blisters on their hands as if they were workers ... what was popular yesterday is not today for the people today are not what they were yesterday".[24]

However, Brecht did not want to replay usual things for the masses, rather courageous and unusual things should be produced for the masses provided they deal with real situations. To him, a realistic work cannot be ascertained simply by checking whether it is like existing works said to be realistic at present or in the past.[25] Thus, he suggests for a 'living', 'combative' and 'truly popular' literature and one must keep pace with the 'rapid development' of social reality.

Within the Marxism, there is a stream of structuralist Marxists wherein Althusser and Goldmann are the leading figures. They were influenced by the mainstream structuralism which views that any individual action or utterance has no meaning apart from the signifying systems that generate it, and thus they receive these structures as timeless and self-regulating systems, whereas the mainstream Marxism considers these structures as historical, changeable and pregnant with contradictions.[26] In fact, Althusser talks of State's Coercive State Apparatus (police, army, etc.) and Ideological State Apparatus (like press, literature, education, etc.). The Ideological State Apparatus has two salient features: (a) It has 'relative autonomy' from the economic base, that is, in everyday life this apparatus functions autonomously and only in the 'ultimate analysis' the economic base determines the ideological state apparatus. (b) It has a class character in the sense that the bourgeois ideology is the dominant ideology in a class society. Althusser is of the view that Marx's theory of knowledge had a 'break' with Hegel. He criticised Hegel's concept of 'totality', which conceives that the essence of the whole is expressed in all its parts. Further, he does not use sociological terms like 'social system' or 'order' because these connote a structure with a 'centre' that determines the form of all its parts. Rather, he talks of 'social formation' suggesting 'decentred' structure. Unlike a living organism, this structure has no governing principle, no originating seed, no overall unity. It implies that various elements or 'levels' within a social formation are not reflections of one essential level (e.g., economic base) – rather the levels have 'relative autonomy' determined by the economic level only 'in the last instance'.[27] Further, unlike some orthodox Marxists, he does not see literature and art merely as a form of ideology (a representation of the imaginary relationship of individuals to their real conditions of existence). Rather, he puts it in between ideology and scientific knowledge. To him, a great literary work neither provides us a proper conceptual understanding of the reality nor merely expresses the ideology of a class. Following Engels' view of Balzac's works, he views that art 'makes us see' a distanced way, 'the ideology from which it is born, in which it bathes, from which it detaches itself as art, and to which it alludes.'[28] Thus, to Althusser, art or literature has the capacity to distance from the ideology that feeds it. In this way, a great literary work can transcend the ideology of the writer.

Another structuralist Marxist is Goldmann who propounded the theory of genetic structuralism. He talks of 'real' and 'potential' consciousness in genetic structuralism. He took this concept from Marx (*The Holy Family)* wherein he argued that the question is not what this or that proletarian thinks or even what the proletarian as a whole think, but is instead the consciousness of the proletarian class. This is the distinction between real and potential consciousness.[29] Goldmann argues that traditionally during the entire history preceding the contemporary societies, man has defined himself in terms of two fundamental dimensions in which his psychic lives and behaviour developed:

(a) the tendency to adapt to the real, and
(b) the tendency to overcome the real towards the possible, that is something beyond which man must create his behaviour.

He finds 'the possible' as the fundamental category for questioning human history.[30] Thus, to him, "Man is greater than what he is because he is always making himself and making a new world".[31] Unlike the traditional literary sociology which conceived the relationship between social life and literary creation in the form of 'things' of collective consciousness of a writer who may reflect it in a transposed manner, Goldmann conceives social life as "ensemble of collective structuration process oriented, as much on the psychic plane as on that of action, towards creating an equilibrium in the relations among men, and between man and Nature. This structuration process is expressed in the psyche of all the group's members ..."[32] In his view, a literary creation fulfils two main functions in social life: (a) "It must not reflect his collective consciousness or merely record reality" rather "creating on the imaginary plane a universe whose content may entirely form that of collective consciousness but whose structure is akin or even homologous to its structuration, it must help man gain the awareness of themselves and of their own affection intellect and practical aspirations."[33] (b) It, at the same time, affords the group members a 'satisfaction' on the imaginary plane which means and can compensate for the multiple frustrations because by the inevitable compromise and inconsistencies which reality imposes: Thus, in his view, the creation of literature, art or philosophy fulfils a collective functioning that is analogous to and very unlike the individual functions of the imaginary at the same time. He was of the view: "Like liberal economy, the universe of the classical novel recognises only one explicit value – the individual and his development in a world at once familiar and strange to him. Thus, the novel is *at once* a biography and a social chronicle."[34]

He criticises positivism stating that sociology must not be positivistic but must take the trans-individual subject into consideration as an actor transforming reality, and the different sectors of the human sciences as dialectical. Those sociologists who look in it for the reflection of collective consciousness rather than for the creation of structures, miss the 'literary fact'.[35] Thus, we find that genetic structuralism of Goldmann tries to combine a grasp of literature as a partly autonomous whole with the specific historical context without reducing it to the epiphenomena. Secondly, his concept of collective consciousness is not merely a reflection of a real collective consciousness that is the result of the tendencies suitable to the consciousness (a dynamic reality) of a particular group. Rather, the relationship between individual literary work and the collective consciousness lies in "the homology of structures – the internal structure of a literary work has a close parallel relation to a particular social structure".[36] Thirdly, literature is not a passive mimesis of an author's class status ('collective subject') nor is the author, as an individual, asked to transcend alienation because as an individual he expresses the aspirations and values of a specific social group. Actually, a group's collective consciousness develops as an outcome of one's activity within the society from his involvement, in political, economic and social life. Thus, there is a praxis and literary creation comes out of the author's group's social activity. Thus, his genetic structuralism perceives literature as a 'creative process' (hence 'genetic'). In his view, an isolated fact is meaningless and it gets a meaning only with reference to whole because the whole and the part are dialectically related. Fourth, he emphasised on the sociological mediations between the author and the novel because society is not atomised rather it comprises different social strata and each class is not homogeneous. He is of the view that creative writers hail from upper and middle classes of society because a literary creation requires both education and leisure – a certain degree of culture that the masses lack. On the one hand, a text reflects the privileged position of the writer but, on the other hand, his text contains a transcendent critical element. That is why Goldmann argues that though the novel of the problematic hero is the novel of a bourgeois society, closely linked with the 'exchange value' in capitalist society, yet it does not accept bourgeois values, rather it comes as a kind of 'critical opposition' or a creative action of resistance to the 'ongoing development of bourgeois society'.

Goldmann has been accused by Swingewood of exploiting Lukacs' idealist theory of the novel, a reversion to the positivism of Taine and the reductionist theories of Plekanov and the later Lukacs, because for him a novel becomes an "unmediated vision of an increasingly alienated society, the writer passively responding to broad socio-economic change. The dialectical relation of writers to social group, culture, society is eliminated in favour of a fatalistic theory of history ..."[37] That is, he has not given due emphasis on super-structure including various kinds of mediations between novel and society, hence economic base directly penetrates into the literary work which has its own autonomous space, not directly corresponding to the 'base'. It is interesting that this has happened, probably unconsciously, while he did talk of 'praxis', 'mediation', 'alienation', 'collective consciousnesses', etc. This is the hidden contradiction in his Marxian structuralist theory of sociology of literature.

Another Marxist sociologist Raymond Williams has developed a 'cultural materialistic' sociological theory of literature. According to him, a literary activity is a part of culture. According to him, there are three kinds of relationship between art and society with emphasis on different aspects:[38]

(a) emphasis on social conditions of art;
(b) emphasis on social material in art works; and
(c) emphasis on social relationship in art works.

As far as *social conditions* of art are concerned, some Marxists emphasise on the origin of typology of art, e.g., Plekhanov (relating art to 'primitive instincts' or drives) or Kautsky (relating the development of art to evolved animal behaviour), or Caudwell (relating art to the 'genotype') and Fischer. Such Marxists have given more weightage to a priori concepts than to the evidence. This position has been correlated to some extent by Mukarovsky and Morawski. Secondly, as a *social material* in art work is concerned, it is more historical and recognises the theory of 'base' and 'superstructure'. Here the basic 'facts' or 'structure' of a given society or a 'historical period' are established by general analysis, and their 'reflection' in art work is directly traced. For instance, both the content and form of the new eighteenth century realistic novel is dependent on the already known facts of social significance of the commercial bourgeoisie. Lukacs takes this position. Thirdly, as far as social relations in art work are concerned, here the idea of 'reflection' is modified or replaced by the idea of 'mediation' which refers "primarily to the necessary process of composition, in a specific medium; as such it indicates the practical relationship between social and artistic forms. But, in its common use, it refers to indirectness of relation between experience and its composition".[39] This indirectness is interpreted differently; for instance, Kafka's novel *The Trial* may be read from different positions:[40] (a) a *mediation by projection* – an irrational and arbitrary social system is indirectly projected as alien; or (b) *mediation by the discovery* of *an objective correlation* – a situation and characters are composed to produce the subject or actual feelings objectively; or (c) *mediation* as *functioning* of *the fundamental social process* of *consciousness in* which some types of crisis that cannot be otherwise directly understood, are 'crystalised' in some direct images and forms of art – such images are fundamental conditions as a general alienation. Here the basic condition means the nature of a whole epoch, a particular society at a particular period or a particular group within a particular society at a particular period. All three conditions, especially second and third, are potentially sociological. Benjamin, Goldmann, Adorno and the Frankfurt School applied this concept of 'mediation' in their works.

Williams further talks of relation between artists and markets as historical production, for the market involves the conception of the work of art as a commodity and of the artist as a specific type of commodity producer.[41]

To Williams, some novels are 'works of art' and others are 'not art' or 'not really art' as the latter are 'pulp fiction', 'commercial trash', 'sub-literature' or 'para-literature'. The third category in between is of 'routine' 'mediocre' or 'lending-library fodder'.[42] In his view, a 'bad novel' does everything that the category of novel connotes but it "fails to do something else, either in its 'aesthetic process' or in terms of its 'seriousness' or its 'relation to reality'.[43]

Williams further observes that realism is not an object "to be identified, pinned down, and appropriated", rather it is a "way of describing certain methods and attitudes".[44] But it is not 'naturalism' – "that unnecessary faithful portrayal of offensive incidents". Strindberg defined naturalism as the 'exclusion of God' and opposed to super-naturalism. Thus, "naturalism in art was reserved to the simple technical reference, while realism, though retaining the elements of this, was used to describe subjects and attitudes to subjects".[45] So Williams explains the realist tradition in fiction as "the kind of novel which creates and judges the quality of a whole way of life in terms of the qualities of persons. The balance involved in this achievement is perhaps the most important thing about it ... it offers a valuing of a whole, a society that is larger than any of the individuals composing it, and at the same time valuing creations of human beings who, while belonging to, and affected by, and helping to define this way of life, are also, in their own terms, absolute ends in themselves. Neither element, neither the society nor the individual, is there as a priority".[46] Thus, Williams gives equal importance to individual and society and clarifies the dialogical and dialectical relationship between the two.[47]

Williams points out two separate traditions of 'social' novel and 'personal' novel: "In the social novel there may be accurate observation and description of the general life, the aggregation; in the personal novel there may be accurate observation and description of persons, the units. But each lacks a dimension, for the way of life is neither aggregation nor unit, but the whole indivisible process".[48] Further, these two types have sub-types. Social novel is of two types – 'documentary' social novel and 'formula' social novel. Documentary or descriptive social novel "creates, as priority, a general way of life, a particular social or working community".[49] It is usually about life in a mining town, in a university or on a merchant ship or on a patrol in Burma; a good documentary is interesting. Yet we miss one dimension: the characters are miners' dons, soldiers' first, illustrations of way of life. This is nearest to the realist novel. On the other hand, in the formula social novel, a "particular pattern is abstracted, from the sum of social experience, and a society is created from this pattern. The simplest examples are in the field of future-story, where the 'future' device ... removes the ordinary tension between the selected pattern and normal observation".[50] Similarly, he divides personal novel into sub-types: documentary and formula. Some of the best (personal descriptive) novels are those which describe subtly selected personal relationships and these are like 'parts' of the realist novel – there is some continuity in the method and substance, e.g., E.M. Forster's *A Passage to India*. Here a society, a general way of living, is apparently there but often a highly personalised landscape to frame an individual portrait rather than a country. So often an imbalance between individual and society occurs, though there is a 'surface of realism': "There is a lack of dimension similar to that in the social descriptive novel, but in a different direction. There the characters were aspects of the society; here the society is an aspect of Characters. The balance we remember is that in which both the general way of life and the individual persons are seen as there and absolute".[51]

In personal descriptive novels, the novelists insist on 'the people as people first, not as social units', but they miss the element of 'common substance', i.e., they do not see people within a society. In personal formula novels, on the other hand, a particular pattern is abstracted from the experience and human individuals are created from that pattern – Joyce's *Portrait of the Artist* is a good example wherein a world is actualised on one man's senses – not narrated but taken as it is lived. Further in Joyce's *Ulysses*, three ways of seeing three worlds, of Stephen, Bloom and Molly, yet the three worlds compose one whole world of the novel. So is the case in Cary's *The Horse's Mouth*, Amis's *That Uncertain*

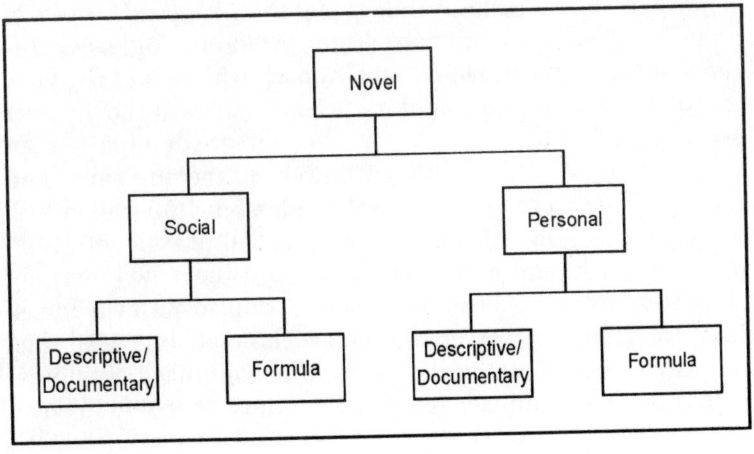

Feeling', and Wain's *Living in the Present*. They begin with many actual feelings but final version of reality is parodic and farcical. Williams' classification of novels is shown graphically in the Figure given above.

To Williams, it is very difficult to write a realist novel in the present era. "The realist novel needs, obviously, a genuine community: a community of persons linked not merely by one kind of relationship – work or friendship or family – but many, interlocking kinds. It is obviously difficult in the twentieth century to find a community of this sort."[52] Hence, the truly creative effort of our time is "the struggle for relationships, of a whole kind, and it is possible to see this as both personal and social: the practical learning of *extending* relationships ... . In the highest realism, society is seen in fundamentally personal terms, and persons, through relationships, in fundamentally social terms. The integration is controlling, yet, of course, it is not to be achieved by an act of will. If it comes at all, it is a creative discovery, and can perhaps only be recorded within the structure and substance of the realist novel."[53]

Williams has also emphasised that the notion of 'hegemony' is very fundamental for the cultural analysis because of its argument that the society has a union of mass activity and practice in shaping the social existence and the domination of politico-economic force in the social world. Thus, this concept is more dynamic, flexible and critical than the crude thesis of economic base and superstructure. Williams borrowed this concept from another Marxist, Gramsci, who was of the view that a new rising class would try to establish its authority over other social classes both by the direct domination of economic, political and military power, on the one hand, and through 'intellectual and moral leadership', on the other. According to him, 'an intense work of cultural penetration' precedes all kinds of revolution because the new emerging class tries to subjugate other social strata to its own ideas. Therefore, he defines a dominant class as one that has saturated society with the spirit of its morality, customs, religious and political practices – thus there is a new

'Weltansauung'. He differentiates between 'hegemony' – associated with equilibrium and consent – and 'domination' – associated with coercion and state power. Thus, hegemony is identified with the 'civil society' institutions like family, church, education, etc. On the other hand, direct domination is identified with the state or 'political society' (army, bureaucracy, police and so on). Gramsci sees superstructure consisting of an 'effective operating reality' and it commands obedience of the subordinate strata.[54] Thus, we find Gramsci's concept of hegemony, being a balance between the elements of force and consent, quite useful in theorising the sociology of literature. Gramsci also found a relationship of the author with the bourgeois classes as there is problematic cause; in his view the bourgeois cannot train its own intellectuals, therefore it takes them from the professional and landed strata. Further, Gramsci was of the view that "all men are intellectuals ... but not all men have in society the function of intellectuals".[55] He distinguished between 'traditional' and 'organic' intellectuals. While the former are in older and more diverse, and, often indirect, class relations, the latter are directly attached to a serving social class (especially rising class).

Another Marxist theorist Terry Eagleton *(Criticism and Ideology)* invokes Althusser's argument against 'empiricism' (the appeal to immediate experience) to show Raymond Williams' inability to make a genuine break into the theory of sociology of literature. His two concepts 'whole way of life' and 'structure of feeling' suggest unwillingness to differentiate theoretically between subjective experience and objective social conditions of this experience.[56] Following Althusser, he argues that criticism must break with its 'ideological prehistory' and become a 'science'. The main problem, to him, is to define the relationship between literature and ideology since, in his opinion, texts do not reflect historical reality, rather work upon ideology to produce an effect of the 'real'. The text may seem to be free in its relation to reality (as it can create a character and a situation at will) but it is not free in its use of ideology. Here ideology refers to systems of representations (aesthetic, religious, judicial, etc.), which shape the mental view of lived experience. Thus, the meanings and perceptions produced in the text are a reworking of ideologies' own working of reality – thus ideology is not a conscious political doctrine. However, Eagleton does not share Althusser's view that literature can distance itself from ideology because it is a complex reworking of existing ideology. But the literary result is not merely a reflection of other ideological discourses, rather a special production of ideology. Therefore, criticism is not concerned with just the laws of literary form or the theory of ideology, but with the laws of the production of ideological discourses as literature.[57] However, in late 1970s, due to the impact of post-structuralist thought, there was a shift in his thought from the 'scientific' attitude of Althusser to the revolutionary thought of Brecht and Benjamin. On the one hand, Eagleton viewed that deconstructive theories (Derrida, Paul de Man, etc.) could be used to undermine all certainties, all fixed and absolute forms of knowledge but, on the other hand, he criticised the deconstruction for its petit bourgeois denial of 'objectivity' and material 'interests' (particularly class interests). This contradictory view was the result of his shift towards Lenin's view that a correct theory "assumes final shape only in close connection with the practical activity of a truly mass and truly revolutionary movement".[58] Thus, the Marxist criticism was now guided by politics, not by philosophy – the critics must break received notions, on 'literature' and reveal their ideological role in shaping the subjectivity of readers. Later, he also appreciated Brecht's radical approach to meaning: "a work may be realist in June and anti-realist in December."[59]

Another Marxist theorist Fredric Jameson (*Marxism and Form,* 1971) has propounded a 'dialectical theory of criticism'. It has following features:[60] First, dialectical criticism does not isolate individual literary works for analysis as an individual is a part of a larger social structure (a tradition or a movement) or a historical situation. Second, the dialectical critic has no preconceived categories to apply to literature rather his categories (style, character, image, etc.) must be understood finally as an aspect of the critics' own historical situation. Third, it seeks to unmask the inner form of genre or body of texts and will work from the surface of a literary work inward to the level where literary form is deeply related to the concrete. Citing from Hemingway, Jameson says that the 'dominant category of experience' in the novels is the process of writing itself. Fourth, Jameson thinks that a narrative is not simply a literary form or mode but an essential 'epistemological category' – social reality presents itself to the human minds only in the form of stories and even a scientific theory is a form of story. Again all narratives need some kind of interpretation and all interpretations are essentially transcendent and ideological. Therefore, at the most, we can use ideological concepts as a means of transcending ideology. Thus, he disagrees with post-structuralists like Deleuze and Guattari ('Anti-oedipus') who attack 'transcendent' (strong) interpretation and favour only 'immanent' interpretation that avoids imposing a strong 'meaning'. To Jameson, even New Criticism immanentist has transcendent interpretation as its master code is 'humanism'. Finally, his notion of 'political unconscious' takes from Freud the concept of 'repression' but turns it from the individual level to the collective level, as the function of ideology is to repress 'revolution'. He says that not only the oppressors require this 'political unconscious' but also the oppressed who would find their existence unbearable if revolution were not repressed. Therefore, to analyse a novel, one needs to establish at first an absent cause ('the not-revolution'); he proposes a critical method that includes three 'horizons' – a level of immanent analysis, a level of social-discourse analysis, and an epochal level of historical reading.[61] Generally, he takes Althusser's notion of social reality as a 'decentred structure' in which theories' levels develop that in relative autonomy and work at different time scales (co-existence of feudal and capitalist time scales).

Another realist, Milan Kundera has written a famous book *The Art of Novel*. It is difficult to put him in a watertight category of Marxist or postmodernist. However, since he talks of existentiality (realist but undogmatic), on the one hand,

and gives due weightage to the 'form' of a literary creation, on the other, he may be called a post-Marxist.[62] His views are as follows: (a) Following Herman Broch, to him the sole *raison d'tre* of a novel is "to discover what only a novel can discover. A novel that does not discover a hitherto unknown segment of existence is immoral. Knowledge is the novel's only morality" (pp. 5–6). He defines a novel: "The great prose form in which an author thoroughly explores, by means of experimental selves (characters), some great themes of existence" (p. 142).

(a) "Novel is Europe's creation – its discoveries belong to the whole of Europe" (p. 6).

(b) "The path of the novel emerges as a parallel history of the Modern Era" (p. 9).

(c) "Totalitarian Truth excludes relativity, doubt, questioning; it can never accommodate ... the *spirit* of *novel*" (p. 14). Novel's spirit is the 'spirit of complexity' – it asks the reader: "Things are not as simple as you think" (p. 9) and 'spirit of continuity' – "each work is an answer to preceding ones, each work contains all the previous experience of the novel. But the spirit of our times is firmly focused on a present that is so expansive and profuse that it shoves the past off our horizon and reduces times to the present moment only. Within this system the novel is no longer a work (thing made to last, to connect the past with the future) but one current event among many, a gesture with no tomorrow" (pp. 18–19).

(d) Novel "cannot live in peace with the spirit of our time: if it is to go on discovering the undiscovered, to go on 'progressing' as novel, it can do so only against the progress of the world" (p. 19).

(e) "All novels, of every age, are concerned with the enigma of the self. As soon as you create an imaginary being, a character, you are automatically confronted by the question: What is the self? How can the self be grasped?" (p. 23).

(f) "A character is not a simulation of a living being. It is an imaginary being. An experimental self. In that way the novel reconnects with its beginnings" (p. 34).

(g) Regarding history, Kundera propounds four principles (pp. 36–38): (i) to behave towards history like the stage designer who constructs an abstract set out of the few items indispensable to the action; (ii) keeping only those historical circumstances that 'create a revelatory existential situation' for characters; (iii) historical events forgotten by historiography – after the 1968 Russian invasion of Czechoslovakia reign of terror against the public was preceded by officially organised massacres of dogs, but it is forgotten by historians though of very anthropological importance; and (iv) not only historical circumstances must create a new existential situation for the character, but history *itself* "must be understood and analysed as an existential situation". To Kundera, "The novelist is neither historian nor prophet: he is an explorer of existence" (p. 44). There is not a history but *histories* of novel (p. 143).

(h) Novel has an extraordinary power of incorporation: "whereas neither poetry nor philosophy can incorporate the novel, the novel can incorporate both poetry and philosophy without loosing thereby anything of its identity, which is characterised ... precisely by its tendency to embrace other genres, to absorb philosophical and scientific knowledge" (p. 64). Novelists express their ideas as "intellectual exercises, paradox games, improvisations, rather than statements of thought" (as philosophers do) (p. 78).

(i) He shares Broch's view that in this age of excessive specialisation, novel is one of the last outposts where man can still maintain connections with life in its entirety (p. 67).

(j) Novel, like music, has polyphony where all voices are equal, none should dominate over others (pp. 74–75).

(k) The novel form is 'almost boundless freedom' (p. 83); but on the other hand, he cautions, "Whenever a novel abandons its themes and settles for just telling the story, it goes flat. A theme ... can be developed on its own, outside the story" (pp. 83–84). He calls this approach to theme 'digression' meaning, 'abandoning the story for a moment' (p. 84). Since theme is an existential inquiry which is the examination of certain words (theme words), novel is primarily based on some 'fundamental words'. To him, all novelists write a kind of *theme* (the first novel) *and variations* (p. 137).

(l) He talks of 'radical autonomy' of novel that allowed Kafka to say things about human condition that no social or political thought could ever tell (p. 117).

(m) Novel is by its very definition 'the ironic art' whose 'truth' is 'concealed, undeclared, undeclarable' (p. 134).

(n) He tells three possibilities for the novelist: (i) to *tell* a story (Fielding), (ii) to *describe* a story (Flaubert), and (iii) to *think* a story (Musil). The nineteenth century novel of description was in harmony with the positivist/scientific spirit of the time (p. 139).

(p) In art, 'form is always more than a form' as every novel gives an answer to: what is human existence and wherein does its poetry lie? (p. 161).

Critical Realism

Frankfurt school of sociology developed 'critical sociology' in general and a theory of critical realism, by synthesising Marxist and Freudian elements, in sociology of literature, in particular. Among them Horkheimer, Adorno, Herbert Marcuse and Leo Lowenthal are noteworthy. Habermas spoke against the attack on cultural modernism by Daniel Bell and other neo-conservatives, and defended the still unrealised potential of the Enlightenment. In his book *The Theory of Communicative Action* (1981), he presents a concept of 'communicative reason'. There is a problem of three cultural spaces that Max Weber distinguished: (a) the theoretical (science), (b) the practical (morality), and (c) the aesthetic (art). According to Habermas, each subject has its own inner-logic that cannot be easily reconciled with those of others. Therefore, we have three different forms of augmentation – empirical-theoretical discourse, moral discourse and aesthetic critique – that is, three different 'rationality complexes'. But these complexes became the monopolies of coteries of experts. Consequently, instead of enriching daily life, as Enlightenment expected, they have distanced themselves from the 'life-world'. Again, under 'capitalist modernisation', the empirical-theoretical or cognitive-instrumental rationality complex has dominated and marginalised other modes of knowing. Thus, it has become a mercenary means-end rationalism that, according to Habermas, deserves post-structuralist charges but it cannot be equated with modernity. He gives language an absolutely central place. In fact, he moves from the prevailing modernist subjectivistic 'philosophy of consciousness' to a 'philosophy of inter-subjectivity', that is, of communication and consciousness that is all-inclusive, where only those are excluded who exclude themselves by rejecting its communicative reason. Here, he differs from deconstructionist avant-gardists (and their supporters like Lyotard). He thinks anti-representationalism emancipatory, as it will bring changes that will bring us closer to the ultimate consensus that communicative reason has enabled, but it can never be an end in itself. Habermas has distinguished three conservative positions:[63]

(a) the 'pre-modernism' of the 'old conservatives' (F.R. Leavis);
(b) anti-modernism' of the 'young conservatives' (Foucault, Derrida, etc.); and
(c) postmodernism' of 'neo-conservatives' (Daniel Bell, etc.).

The neo-conservatives accept the finality of the separation of the spheres of science, morality and art from each other and from the life-world. They accept the ascendancy of functional rationality (at the expense of morality) on the level of social organisations (politics). Since they have given up the project of modernity, in Habermas' opinion, they are the only true postmodernists. The 'young conservatives' have not moved beyond the modernity project at all. Rather they recapitulate the basic experience of aesthetic modernity.

Lowenthal has written a lot on sociology of literature. He considers a sociological analysis of literature as helping in aesthetic experience of literature. His views may be summarised as follows.[64] Instead of focusing on contemporary literature (that is only one of many sources to know the contemporary period), he focusses on the great creations of the past, since he thinks literature as the best source of knowing that period and for this he searches society in the literature. Second, literature is the historical store of deep individual experiences – of love and nature – which are influenced by social contexts. Third, an author does not depict reality fully objectively, rather either he supports it or opposes it. Thus, the experience of reality and one's perspective to it is more important than merely depiction of reality. Fourth, contrary to Walter Benjamin's view (that in history the voice of the winners is dominant), the voice of the defeated and a desire of their victory is reflected in a true art. Fifth, ideology is essentially a false consciousness, an illusion that covers the social reality with a mask of mystery and transforms it – thus it makes it difficult to understand the contradictions of a capitalist society. Sixth, there is an essential internal and indivisible unity between form and content. He agrees with Adorno's notion of inner criticism of art. Seventh, the form of a creation is determined by the fact that how it is grasped and experienced. He, unlike empiricists, analyses the *class base* of a creation in production process, *social context* in the distribution process and *readers' grasp* in consumption process of literature. Finally, popular literature is a good source of understanding the consciousness of people and the value system of modern age.

But he did not differentiate between genuine people's literature/culture and mass literature/culture. Secondly, in his later writings, he talks of man, European man and philosophical communities of writers in place of class and ideology. Thus his perspective becomes narrowed.

Marcuse[65] talks of one-dimensional man in modern age of capitalism that is a mass society, mass culture and mass art. Consequently, the culture is reduced to an industry, instead of a creation, and such a society of alienation destroys the autonomy of culture, art and individual's critical consciousness and imagination.

Similarly, Adorno too takes a critical view of reality. Criticising Lukacs' view of realism, Adorno argued that art (including literature), unlike the mind, does not have a direct contact with the reality, rather an art is set apart from reality; hence, detachment provides it significance and power.

Secondly, he argued, art cannot reflect the social system, rather acts within that as an irritant and thus produces an indirect kind of knowledge that can be achieved by writing difficult experimental (not directly polemical) texts: "Art is the negative knowledge of the actual world."[66] Thirdly, the commercialisation of culture (e.g., music, cinema, advertising) destroys the listener's ability to appreciate the formal unity of a classical work, on the one hand, and compels the composer to respond by producing fragmented music or cinema or advertising, in which the grammar of musical language (tonality) is denied, on the other. Thus, commercialisation results into the cheapening of art.

Theory of Post-structuralism/Postmodernism

The term 'postmodern' (like modernism) has different connotations to different persons.[67] For instance, in the field of dance criticism, according to Sally Banes, it refers both to an 'early' movement towards "functionality, purity and self-reflexibility" and later "also to rekindling of interest in narrative structures". Secondly, in the field of photography, 'content' is associated with realism and modernism, whereas postmodern age is associated with anti-representational, anti-narrative and deconstructive photography of Cindy Sherman, Sherry Levine and Richard Prince. Thirdly, in the field of architecture, the 'postmodern' referred to the vernacular and history – reinforcing a humanising narrative. For most of the American critics, postmodernism has moved away from narrative and representation – a move towards a radical aesthetic autonomy towards a pure formalism. Therefore, due to these differences in meaning of the term 'postmodern', Hans Bertens says, "Depending on the artistic discipline then, postmodernism is either a radicalisation of the self-reflexive movement within modernism, a turning away from narrative and representation, or an explicit return narrative and representation, and sometimes, it is both".[68]

However, as he further explains, in 1960s – the period of counter-culture – postmodernism was perceived as "attitude of modern culture or a new eclectic and radically democratic sensibility" rejecting the exclusivist and repressive character of liberal humanism and its institutions. Lesly Fedler identified this view. But, in 1970s, postmodernism entered into post-structuralism, taking inspirations from Roland Barthes, Jacques Derrida, Michel Foucault, Jacques Lacan, Gilles, Deleuze and Felix. Like post-structuralism, postmodernism also rejects the empirical idea that language can represent reality. It gives up the rational function of the language and shares the principle of post-structuralism that 'language constitutes', rather than reflects the world and, therefore, knowledge is usually distorted by the language – by the historical situation and specific environment in which it grows. The postmodern subject is thus largely 'other-determined' whereas the subject of the modernity was autonomous, objectively rational and self-determined.

Further, in late 1970s and early 1980s, the post-structuralist postmodernism of Barthes and Derrida was linguistic, that is, textual, in orientation. Their attack on functionalist notions of knowledge, representation and the subject is combined with a strong emphasis on 'free-play' (Derrida) and inter-textuality. Barthes talked of the 'Death of the Author' (1968).[69] Rejecting the traditional view that the author is the origin of the text, source of its meaning, and the only authority for its interpretation, he says that reader is free to read the text from any direction as there is no correct route. He saw the text as a 'multidimensional phase' in which a variety of writings, none of them original, bled and clashed, and has a "tissue of quotations drawn from the innumerable centres of culture".[70] He and his colleagues thus talk of the end of representation – that is, the language fails to represent anything outside itself, on the one hand, and there is the death of the subject, on the other.

Further, he sees literature as a special, semantic system aiming to put 'meaning' into the world, but not 'a meaning' as a literary work is neither quite meaningless (mysterious or 'inspired') nor ever quite clear – rather it is 'suspended' meaning. So the great literary work has a power "to ask questions of the world" – its ideologies, beliefs, common sense – without giving any answers because no great work is 'dogmatic', hence such work is interpreted and reinterpreted continuously. So the literature is a system of signs and its being lies 'not in the message but in the system'; similarly critic's task is not to reconstitute the message of the work, but only its system. Finally, he argues that a meta-language can be "objective and subjective, historical and existential, totalitarian and liberal". The language used by the critic does not come from heaven but is "offered by his situation in time" and it is the "latest stage of a certain historical development of knowledge, ideas, and intellectual passions; it is a necessity". On the other hand, each critic chooses this necessary language, in accordance with a certain existential pattern, as the means of exercising an intellectual function which is his, and his alone, putting into the operation his 'deepest self'. In this way the critical work contains within itself a dialogue between two historical situations and two subjectivities, those of the author and those of the critic.[71]

In the second stream of post-structuralist postmodernism in 1980s, M. Foucault and J. Lacan accepted the reality of the textuality and signs, of representations that do not represent but they emphasised on the power, and the constitution of the subject. In their view, knowledge that was neutral and objective to the positivists, and politically emancipatory to the left, is necessarily bound up with power, and hence suspect. It questions the very power inherent in the knowledge and language and the discourse surrounding us. It tries to undo the institutionalised hierarchies and hegemony of a single discursive system in its advocacy of 'difference', 'pluriformity', and 'multiplicity'. This stream of postmodernism stands for the 'other' – women, people of colour, non-heterosexuals and children. It also looks into the ways in which human beings are constituted by discourses, i.e., by language, and recognise themselves as subjects. Foucauldian postmodernism had a democratising influence within cultural institutions and in the humanities. This redefinition of postmodernism in 1980s brought it close to feminism and multi-culturalism that are now associated with postmodernism.[72]

The commodification of late capitalism, in view of F. Jameson and J. Baudrillard, has obliterated Marxist distinction between the economic (base) and the cultural (superstructure), rather an indeterminate situation has arisen where the economic and cultural create and feed each other. Actually, industrial production has given way to Baudrillard's 'Semiurgy' – the sinister production of signs.[73] However, existential postmodernist William Spanos argued that the criticism can make 'a difference in the world!' and for this commitment, existential subject is required. He refused the priority of language. For him postmodernism "is not fundamentally a chronological event but rather a permanent mode of understanding".[74] In the postmodernist debate, in Bertens' view, Habermas and Jameson participated for the traditional left, Baudrillard for the radical left, and Lyotard and Rorty for the domesticated postmodernism. J.F. Lyotard, like Alain Touraine, Daniel Bell, etc., talks of the replacing of manufacturing of material goods by the information as a central concern in the most advanced economies, and in his view 'computerisation of society' will affect the nature of knowledge which has become 'an informational commodity'; science has been forced to abandon its original integrity and has become an instrument in the hands of power. Like Habermas, in Lyotard's analysis also, the instrumental rationality has dominated other forms of reason. In Lyotard's analysis, however, the social and the political are relegated to the background. His point of departure is the demise of 'meta-narratives'; he defines postmodern as 'incredulity towards meta-narratives'. These meta- or grand-narratives are the transcendent and universal truths that function to give Western civilisation an objective legitimation. Following Wittgenstein, Lyotard says that these meta-narratives have been replaced by a great number of 'language games' – ranging from Wittgenstein's 'models of discourse', i.e., various forms of utterance (denotative, performative, prescriptive, etc.) following, specific set of rules, via the discourses employed by social institutions and professions, to full-scale narratives (or little narratives).[75]

In the stream of anti-theoretical radicalism, Robert Rorty thinks that what is required is a 'detheoreticised sense of community'. He finds Lyotard right in his rejection of meta-narratives as well as Habermas' 'universalistic philosophy' (his search for communicative rationality) but he finds Habermas right in his insistence on 'liberal politics' which the post-structuralists want to give up in order to avoid universalistic philosophy. Thus, Rorty takes a middle position between Lyotard and Habermas. In his work *The Mirror of Production* (1975) Baudrillard links power with the language and observations that consumer products should function within a differential sign system that programmes individual consumption, i.e., "the system of consumption is based on a code of signs (object/signs) and differences, not on need and pleasure.[76] He does not deny needs but argues that consumption has a system of meaning and is not organised along line of needs and pleasure. He further argues: "All the repressive and reductive strategies of power systems are already present in the internal logic of the sign, as well as those of exchange value and political economy."[77] Therefore, our only hope is 'total revolution' if we desire to restore 'the symbolic' (meaning). But this is not the proletarian revolution. In fact, he subordinated the political economy (based on production) to a general political economy of the sign (based on consumption). Thus, he abandoned his earlier Marxism. He prefers a Nietzschean aesthetic of aristocratic disdain and excess to the suffocating politics of rationalism and utilitarianism that Marxism has in common with its archenemy. To him, the notion of mode of production has become irrelevant in a world dominated by 'a mode of signification' that, in turn, is controlled by the 'code'.[78] Thus, in the hyper-real, the idea of representation has become irrelevant. Labour, production, the political, everything persists but lacks all referentiality and is reduced to the status of meaningless sign. But Baudrillard did not define terms like 'code' and he lacks a systematic analysis. Secondly, he ignores the evidence such as benefits from new media in providing vital information to the people and counteracting parochialism with humanising images of others. Thirdly, he does not see the importance of economy, state, race and gender domination and wrongly takes contemporary trends as finalities.[79]

J. Derrida talks of deconstruction of hierarchy (speech-writing) and points out that speech implies writer's immediate presence, but the writing does not do so and the latter can be repeated (printed), hence reinterpreted. Therefore, writing is secondary and threatens to contaminate, supplement or even takes the place of speech because speech is always already written.[80] However, says Eagleton, Derrida's deconstruction wrongly denies material (class) interests, though it rightly questions fixed and absolute forms of knowledge.[81]

Another theorist, Fredric Jameson, who has taken elements of postmodernism in Marxism, is of the view that there has been an erosion of the older distinction between high culture and so-called mass or popular culture.[82] Like Baudrillard, he finds a causal relationship between new developments in western capitalism and the rise of the postmodern. It is a "new society of the media or the spectacle, or multinational capitalism".[83] It is characterised by new consumption patterns, by an ever faster turnover in the areas of fashion and styling, by planned obsolescence, by the forceful presence of advertising and the mass media (especially television), by the explosion of small towns (at the expenses of both the city and country), by the demands of standardisation, by the arrival of automobile culture, etc., especially in the late 1940s and early 1950s in USA, with the establishment of the Fifth Republic in France in 1958. Thus, he sees postmodernism in terms of periodisation as did Lyotard and Baudrillard. The deeper logic of the new social system, with its key element of perpetual change, has led to the disappearance of a 'sense of history' in the culture, to a 'pervasive depthlessness', to a 'perpetual present' from where the memory of tradition has disappeared. In postmodern art, that deeper logic surfaces two features of 'pastiche' (blank parody) and schizophrenic discontinuity. The former arrives when as a result of radical fragmentation we have "nothing but stylistic diversity and heterogeneity".[84] He discusses schizophrenic discontinuity in terms of Lacan's view of schizophrenia as a language disorder resulting from the subject's failure "to accede fully into the realm of speech and language". Thus, his postmodernism is the "transformation of reality into images", the "fragmentation of time into a series of perpetual presents".[85] To him, pastiche and radical discontinuity were elements within 'modernism proper' but their place was only marginal – not central – whereas they occupy the central position in contemporary cultural production. He also sees the postmodern as a profound crisis in representation. History has disappeared and the present has dissolved in images. However, unlike Lyotard who saw anti-representationism as a necessary defensive manoeuvre against the terror of representational consensus, Jameson argues about the impossibility of representation as the end of an emancipatory politics.

Later, in his article 'Post Modernism or the Cultural Logic of Late Capitalism',[86] he sees postmodernism "dialectically as catastrophe and progress all together". Now he proposes a new concept of 'cognitive mapping' – a new representational practice – that is nothing but a code word for 'class consciousness'. Jameson shares Marxist representation of history as a story of class struggle, hence issues of gender, race and ethnicity are not significant in his theorising. His thesis also draws on Althusser's conception of semi-autonomy and, on the other hand, he borrows from anti-Marxist post-structuralists – the notion of schizophrenia from Lacan, Deleuze and Guattari, 'intensities' and the 'sublime' from Lyotard, the 'simulacrum' from Deleuze and Baudrillard, and the idea of 'homeopathic' strategy from Baudrillard (as a version of the latter's fatal strategies) To him, the lack of depth or 'superficiality' is the 'supreme formal feature' of postmodernism. Under postmodernism, feelings become, in Lyotard's term, 'intensities', in that they "are now free-floating and impersonal and tend to be dominated by a peculiar kind of euphoria".[87] Later, Jameson followed Ernst Mandel's concept of 'Late Capitalism' (1978) in the periodisation: the first period of market capitalism and its aesthetic corrolary 'realism'; second period of monopoly or imperialist capitalism which gave rise to modernism; third period – and current one – of late capitalism that corresponds to the postmodern aesthetic. In the current period, there is an expansion of capital into hitherto uncommodified areas. Especially in the West, the late capitalism has penetrated and commodified representation ('the media') itself. However, according to Mike Davis (1985) modernism, at least in architecture remained "the functional aesthetic of late capitalism".[88] It is a strong criticism against Jameson. To Jameson, technology of our own moment – the computer, the television set, and other machines of reproduction rather than of production – no longer possess the 'capacity for representation' that characterised the technologies of capitalism's earlier stages.

Secondly, Jameson's focus on class struggle as centre of political struggle, i.e., working class as the agent par excellence of progressive change, is not proved in all societies at all times.

Thirdly, he does not see the significance of feminist, ethnic and ecological politics which is very significant in present time.

There is one more stream, called 'post-colonialism', pioneered by Edward Said who is of the view that the history of cultural practice in Europe and USA carries within it "the unequal relationship of force between the outside western ethnographer-observer and a primitive, or at least different but certainly weaker and less developed, non-Western society.'[89] Hence, in Third World literature, there is a post-colonial effort "to reclaim traditions, histories, and cultures from imperialism, and it is also a way of entering the various world discourses on an equal footing".[90] Further, he points out that "to see Other not as ontologically given but as historically constituted would be to erode the exclusivist biases we so often ascribe to cultures, our own not least".[91]

From the above discussion about postmodernism, following major tenets of postmodern theory of sociology of literature are noteworthy:

(a) Language 'constitutes' rather than represents the reality; there is a crisis in representation – loss of faith in our ability to represent the real;

(b) The autonomous and stable subject of modernity is replaced by a postmodern agent whose identity is generally *other-determined* and always in process;

(c) Meaning has become local, social, contingent/provisional and self-sufficient; there are meanings and interpretations, rather than one meaning and one interpretation;

(d) Knowledge only counts as such within a given discursive form, that is, a given power structure. According to Brian McHale, the epistemological orientation of modernism – its overriding interest in *knowing* – is giving way to the ontological orientation of postmodernism – its interest in *modes of being*;[92]

(e) Charging modernism to be anthropocentric, Eurocentric, repressive, reductive, rationalist, elitist and intellectually self-deceptive, postmodernism (especially anti-modernism stream) presents itself as liberating, democratic, open, respectful to both the human and non-human, and sensitive to desire;

(f) It questions the 'universalistic' grand narratives like Marxism and liberalism as it is not feasible to have a universal theory for all societies and all times;

(g) It also questions the history, and gives more importance to the present;

(h) It gives more importance to difference, plurality and diversity;

(i) It asks *questions* rather than provides answers; further it focusses on the differences between what a text says and what it thinks it says; and

(j) It deconstructs the text.

However, postmodernism is not without criticism. It deconstructs text in order to analyse but forgets to reconstruct it. Secondly, though grand theorisation is not possible in every arena of social life yet in some cases it can be reasonably done, at least 'middle range' theorisation (as Robert K. Merton says) is possible. Thirdly, the role of history cannot be denied for proper understanding of literature in particular and society in general. It wrongly rejects modernism totally because it is relevant, though not in westernised form, to traditional developing countries like India where the modernity project is still incomplete.

As discussed above, several theories of sociology of literature have perceived literature, especially novel, in different ways. However, one finds these theories often overemphasising one or more aspects of social reality at the cost of other aspects. Therefore. creative and critical elements of sociology of literature are emphasised here, especially with reference to the analysis of Hindi novels.

First, the relationship between the literature and society is not direct, easy, one-dimensional and causal, rather it is a multidimensional, complex, complicated, indirect and associational. In fact, there are several 'mediations' between literature and society, like author's socialisation, especially in family, formal education, occupational experience, participation in a social, cultural, economic or political movement, his earlier writings, his interaction with readers, demands of market through publishers, sharing of others' consciousness, etc., as these articulate in some way or other his values and it has an indirect influence on his literary works. As Leon Trotsky rightly says: "artistic creativity is a very complex web which is not woven automatically ... but comes into being from complex interrelations ...".[93] In fact, the relationship between literature and society is of complex nature in terms of correspondence, interaction, interdependence, tension, cooperation and conflict, hence a two-way dynamic and dialectical dialogue. Here, we do not see a deterministic relationship between a literary work and the external world.

Actually, a text (novel) is seen here in a context – social, political, cultural, economic and historical: for instance, a novel written during freedom struggle of India needs to be linked, at least indirectly, to the freedom struggle being the major epochal reality to have influenced the novels of the time.

Second, the 'tragic vision' of the author is considered important for the analysis of a literary work because it decides whether he takes literature as a medium of human liberation and collective empowerment or just pursues as an art for art's sake. That is, the deep insight of a genuine literary creation actually raises certain questions about the existing system or its functioning. Hence, one needs to analyse whether there is a coherence between the world vision of the novel and the world vision of the society at a particular time. For this very purpose, one is to analyse three levels of social reality in the Hindi world: (a) political structure which is liberal-democratic with rational individualism; (b) economic structure that is a mixed economy with the co-existence of state and market; and (c) social structure, especially hierarchised Hindu social structure in which dalits are ranked at the bottom. Actually, Hindu social structure was broken by the colonialism, on the one hand, and refined on the other. Therefore, it fragmented and different religious groups' vision was distorted. Thus, there are contradictions between different visions due to social forces of continuity and change. In fact, group contradictions have increased over the years and there is a confrontation of group contradictions with the core values of liberal democracy (individualism, rationalism and market). Therefore, individual facts and events are to be examined in relation to the structural unity. In India, these three levels of reality are competing with one another, therefore it becomes very difficult for any novelist to decide as to which level is dominant.

Third, it is very significant to analyse as to whether the novelist has been successful to understand the social reality in depth and whether there is its deep expression in his novel rather than superficially depicting the *details* covering a wider range in unilinear dimension vertically. This is so because a person's self-experience need not be sufficient. It becomes sufficiently authentic only when the novelist understands, through a genuine empathy, the complex social reality in depth with a genuine vision and clear perspective to support or oppose a particular reality. Therefore, in the analysis of a text or a good novel, one needs to see whether the novelist has been able to express what he wanted to express artistically and creatively or not. However, more significant is the fact as to why a particular novel has been written and why it is read by the people.

Fourth, as far as the relationship between form and content of a novel is concerned, it is neither static nor deterministic, unilinear and causal. Rather it is dialogical, dynamic and dialectical. Message (content) and medium (form) are to be analysed sensibly. Novel by its very nature requires newness or 'discovery' in form or content, or style or language or plot. It is emphasised here that in a novel, form is more than a form. Its narrative may be macro or micro depending on the characters, theme and situation. Thus, some form of a linkage between the local and global/national is to be grasped from the novels.

Fifth, in the context of Indian literature, it is necessary to see that how colonialism and struggle against it are depicted in Indian novels, especially those written in that period.

Finally, it is also significant to see as to how the 'others' or marginals, dalits in India, are represented in the novels in the larger context – with empathy or sympathy. That is, whether they are shown to accept the hegemony of the upper classes and castes or to challenge it manifestly or latently. One has to see novelist's vision regarding diversity and plurality. That is to say, cultural diversity is as much needed for humankind as biodiversity. Needless to say that a literary creation is a cultural action for freedom in the ultimate analysis.

Notes and References

1. These types are: (a) 'sociologically aware' study of literature: here the focus is on the literary work, not on the sociological problems.

Actually such social critics refer to the social coordinates and conditions of the literary work. For instance, they use the concept of 'alienation' in their literary works. For instance, Malcolm Bradley takes this position in his work *Social Context of Modern English Literature* (1971); (b) literary work as a 'kind of sociology': here literary work is focused as a source of data, or as a carrier of human values or as new information about social institutions. For instance, Lewis Coser in his work *Sociology Through Literature* (1963) shows that social life could be understood by analysing literary works with the help of concepts like role, anomie, bureaucracy and deviance. Similarly, Joan Rockwell shows in her work *Fact in Fiction* (1974) that language is the significant mechanism of social transformation; (c) 'social genesis' of literature: this view perceives as to how literature arises in a society, that is, social forces affect a literary work. Here literature is seen as social facts or contradictions (including structuralism, and some forms of historical materialism) or as the symbolic transformation of social reality (semiotics). This approach overemphasises the social genesis at the cost of unique creativity and imaginative power of the author. For instance, David Caute accuses Goldmann for reducing the author to merely a 'midwife' to help at the birth of literary work; (d) literary work 'may affect society': this approach believes that a literary work brings in social change, though indirectly and slowly. For instance, Bertolt Brecht emphasises this positive aspect of a literary work and argues that socialists must use the literary works for social transformation; (e) literary work as both 'social product and social force': this conception perceives literary work as a creative product of society as well as a social force leading to social change by providing political education. Writers like Terry Eagleton, Walter Benjamin, Sartre and Raymond Williams have taken this position of dialectical relationship between literary works and society in a historical way. For details, see Jane Routh and Janet Wolff (1977), 'Introduction', in *The Sociology of Literature: Theoretical Approaches*, University of Keele, Staffordshire.

2. Manager Pandey (1989), *Sahitya Ke Samaj Shastra Ki Bhumika*, Haryana Sahitya Akademi, Chandigarh, pp. 117–19.

3. Alan Swingewood (1975), *The Novel and Revolution*, Macmillan Press, London, p. 7.
4. M. Pandey, op. cit., pp. 123–29.
5. Cited in Raman Selden (1985), *Contemporary Literary Theory*, The Harvester Press, Sussex, p. 8.
6. They also influenced the development of New Criticism in America during 1940s and 1950s. They treated literature as a special use of knowledge that gets its distinctiveness by deviating from and distorting 'practical' language (as used in daily life). They identify 'literariness' with 'poeticalness', that is, poetry is quintessentially a literary use of language due to its 'constructed' quality – that is, rhythm. Shklovsky used a new concept of 'defamiliarisation' (making strange) in this regard. He wrote in his book *Art as Technique* (1917): "The purpose of art is to impart the sensation of things as they are perceived, and not as they are known. The technique of art is to make objects 'unfamiliar', to make forms difficult, to increase the difficulty and length of perception, the process of perception is an aesthetic end in itself and must be prolonged. *Art is a way of experiencing the artfulness of an object: the object is not important*" (Selden, 1985, p. 10). Thus, these formalists emphasised more on technique of presentation of a perspective rather than common perspective. They cited 18th century British writers like Laurence Stern and Jonathan Swift in their support. However, two concepts of 'defamiliarisation' (Shklovsky) and 'laying bare' (actual process of presentation) influenced Brecht's concept of 'alienation effect'. Similarly, Jakobson used the term 'the dominant' as the 'focussing component of a work of art: it rules, determines and transforms the remaining components' (ibid., p. 15). The concept of defamiliarisation implied change and historical development. Jakobson was of the view that the poetic forms change as a result of a 'shifting dominant', that is, there is a continuing shift in the mutual relationship among the various components in a poetic system. He further added that the poetics of a specific period may be governed by the dominant that is derived from a non-literary system. For instance, the dominant of Renaissance poetry was derived from the visual art, Romantic poetry oriented towards music, and realism's dominant is verbal

art. Thus, he takes into account the *social external reality* whereas the early formalism of Shklovsky did not recognise it.

7. Bakhtin also talked of 'carnivalisation' to describe the shaping effect of carnival on literary genres. For instance, Socrates' dialogue in *The Republic* (at least in the beginning) is carnivalistic as a provoker of argument, where Socrates was a midwife rather than an author of truth. But later, his image of teacher emerges. While the early formalists recorded text as an 'organic unity', Bakhtin's notion on carnival questions the organic unity by emphasising that major literary works may be multi-levelled and resistant to unification. Consequently, the position of author becomes less important in relation to his literary work. However, unlike Roland Barthes, he does not radically question the role of author absolutely, though, like him, he also prefers liberty and pleasure to authority and decorum. Thus, while Shklovsky talked of the text as a unit of device and Tynyanov talks of the text as a functioning system, Bakhtin talks of text as multi-levelled and polyphonic. Another formalist critic Mukarovsky emphasises that extra-literary factors should not be excluded from critical analysis, rather there should be focus on dynamic tension between the literature and society. He talked of 'aesthetic function' – the same object may possess several functions: for example, church may be both a place of worship and a work of art; a stone may be a doorstop, a missile, a building material or an object of art. Thus, we find that a stream of formalists (Shklovsky) emphasised on technical device within the inner world of a literary work, while the other stream of formalists (Jakobson, Bakhtin, Mukarovsky) emphasised on the external world of reality as much as inner world of a literary creation.
8. Cited in A. Swingewood, op. cit., p. 8.
9. Raman Selden, op. cit., pp. 26–27.
10. A. Swingewood, op. cit., p. 9.
11. Karl Marx (1971), *A Contribution to the Critique of Political Economy*, Progress Publishers, Moscow, p. 21.
12. Cited in A. Swingewood, op. cit., pp. 11–12.
13. Cited in R. Selden, op. cit., pp. 28–29.
14. Cited in A. Swingewood, op. cit., p. 6.

15. A. Swingewood, op. cit., p. 17.
16. Bertolt Brecht (1977), 'Against Georg Lukacs', in Ronald Taylor (ed.), *Aesthetics and Politics*, NLV, London, p. 69.
17. M.H. Abrams (1993), *Glossary of Literary Terms*, Prism Books Pvt. Ltd., Bangalore, p. 243.
18. Ibid.
19. B. Brecht, op. cit., p. 79.
20. Ibid., p. 81.
21. Ibid., p. 82.
22. Ibid.
23. Ibid., p. 83.
24. Ibid., pp. 82–83.
25. Actually, he points out: "In each case one must compare the depiction of life in a work of art with the life itself that is being depicted, instead of comparing it with another depiction. Where popularity is concerned, there is one extremely formalistic procedure of which one must beware. The intelligibility of a literary work is not guaranteed merely if it is written exactly like other works which were understood in their time. These other works which were understood in their time were also not always written like the works before them. Steps had been taken to make them intelligible. In the same way, we must do something for the intelligibility of new works today. There is not only such a thing as being popular there is also the process of *becoming popular*" (ibid., p. 85).
26. R. Selden, op. cit., p. 38.
27. Ibid., pp. 39–40.
28. Cited in R. Selden, op. cit., p. 40.
29. L. Goldmann (1977), *Cultural Creation in Modern Society*, Basin Blackwell, Oxford, p. 32. Thus, in a conversation there is not only a man or a device emitting information and a mechanism transmitting it but also a human being who receives it. According to him, the "structure of consciousness requires that certain messages be developed and transmitted, that others be distorted and that the elaboration and transmission of whole series of messages conflicting with the realism of those ends be obstructed. Of course, these three categories of information do

not coincide from one group to another which indicates the extreme complicity involved in studying transmission of messages bearing on the different aspects of human life" (ibid., p. 37). He points out that there are three periods in the history of Western capitalism. First was liberal capitalism which was an individualist period extending up to 1910. During this period the idea of ensemble as totality tends to disappear from consciousness. During this period, two forms of radical individualist philosophy like rationalism and empiricism emerged in the arena of thought, whereas in the literary arena this period was expressed, by the classical novel – that is, the novel of the 'problematic' character. But the classical novel is not homologous to empiricism or to rationalism or to enlightenment philosophy rather it is a critical literary form implying a positive element, that is, the affirmation to the individual and of individual value implicit in the novels of this period from *Don Quixot* to *The Red and the Black* to *Madame Bovary*. However, such novels are a significant social critique. The second period was imperialistic period of capitalism in crisis, around 1910–11; First World War began in 1914 and Second World War occurred during 1939–45 and in between there was depression during 1929–33. Due to the above crises, the mechanism of revolution through the market, necessary for the liberal economy, was disrupted by the development of monopolies, trusts and the new mechanism had emerged. This period conserved individualistic elements but such elements were centred not on individual possibilities (reason or perception) but on his limits – a limit par excellence, death. Existentialism in this period also focussed on the anguish; for instance, Kafka, Musil, Sartre and Camus were extentialist novelists who highlighted the problem of character. However, on the other hand, there was also an attempt to replace the character with the collectivity and to write the novel with collective characters. For instance, Martin du Gard's *The Thivaults*, Mann's *Buddenbrooks*, Galsworthy's *The Forsyte Saga* and the novel of the revolutionary communist Malraux's *Man's Fat*. However, in Goldmann's view, it was a transitional phase. The socialist revolution did not actually change the Western society, the collectivity was not a force able to change it, nor did the novel of the collectivity become a predominant literary form. Third period is the present period of organised capitalism characterised by a consumer society, mass society, organisational capitalism, technocratic society. This period has found a conscious mechanism of self-regulation. According to Goldmann, in the liberal period, man's everyday thought had completely lost sight of the 'totality' (the offer of history, society, production as a whole, etc.). They did not see anything beyond the individual: Homoeconomicus in economics, the Cartesian ego in philosophy, the autonomy of individual consciousness, reason and perception in psychology, and the novel hero in literature. On the other hand, in organisational capitalism, the awareness of 'totality' appears to be the fundamental phenomenon.

30. He says, "The great difference between positivists and dialectical sociology consists precisely in the fact that whereas the former is content to develop the most exact and meticulous possible photography of the existing society, the latter tried to isolate the potential consciousness in the society it studies: the potential developing tendencies oriented toward overcoming the society. In short, the first tries to give an account of the functioning of the existing structuration and the second centres on the possibilities of a theory and transforming social consciousness and reality" (ibid., p. 57).

31. Ibid., pp. 56–57.

32. Ibid., p. 76.

33. Ibid., p. 77.

34. Ibid., p. 79. But Goldmann questions various types of dualities between philosophy and science, and between theory and praxis. For him, "Facts are *constructed*, first within the thought process and already in perception ... . But even outside immediate perception up to the most elaborate theories, the facts are constructions; these constructions, however, are not arbitrary: they have a reason for existing and are founded on the possibility of orientation of helping to comprehend and transform the work; they are not mere givens external to the thinkers. The concept of the subject, of course, has the same status as of their scientific concepts: it is a construction, but a grounded one" (ibid., p. 92). Goldmann is also of the view that since 'what people say does not simply correspond to what they do', therefore a social group's

behaviour should rightly be judged by asking individuals 'what do you think'? And it confuses consciousness with overall functionality. He terms this as an empiricist method that never allows comprehension of reality of phenomena.

35. Ibid., p. 107. In this regard, his two categories are significant. The principle idea of dialectical thought is the category of 'totality'. In his view, history of ideas forms a part of the history of facts: "Totality is the idea that a phenomenon can be comprehended only by first inserting it in the broader structure of which it is a part and in which it has a functioning, the latter being its objective meaning independently of whether or not the men acting, creating it, are conscious of it" (ibid., p. 112). Second, the "identity of subject and object is partial (though to Hegel it is total) because if humanity is historical, if the subjects of action, creation and praxis are social groups (Marx specifies them as social classes), if social groups are collective subjects, then all thought about history and society is science and consciousness; and the group which is thinking is the subject and object of thought" (ibid.). He further explains that "theories, judgments of fact, can be founded only on value judgments, and that value judgment can be founded only on judgments of fact: that they cannot be separated nor can subject and object to be separated" (ibid.). Thus, Goldmann is against positivism. He even asserts that when Mehring, Plekhanov, Kautsky, Bernstein and Lenin (when he wrote *Materialism and Empiriocriticism*) were writing, Marxism was just as positivistic as academic science. Unlike the grand narrative of Marxism with universal typology, Goldmann wants to create a *"localised historical typology"* of different phases in the history of the workers' movement, of the corresponding bureaucracies, and of the present situation of the bureaucracy (ibid., p. 121). However, according to him, dialectics does not signify to judge possibilities morally – desiring democracy or revolution – but in asking what the 'real forces of transformation' are and how the 'subject of the transformation' can be found in reality, in the object, in society (ibid., p. 122).
36. Ibid., p. 79.
37. A. Swingewood, op. cit., pp. 28–29.

38. Raymond Williams (1981), *Culture*, Fontana Paperback, Glasgow, p. 21.
39. Ibid., p. 24.
40. Ibid.
41. Ibid., pp. 44–47. There are three phases of commodity production: (a) Artisanal: independent producer offers his art work for direct sale as he is totally dependent on the immediate market though his work remains 'under his own direction'; (b) Post-artisanal: it has two sub-stages; first, the producer sells his art work to a *distributive* intermediary who becomes his occasional employer; second, the producer sells his art work to a *production* intermediary, and capitalist social relation exists there because the intermediary purchases it for the sake of profit and he has direct relation with the market; for instance, the booksellers evolve into publishers; (c) Market professional: In literature, due to complex situation, there is both increasing capitalisation of productive intermediaries – modern publishers and increasing professionalisation among writers. Two indicators of such changing relations are 'copyright' and 'royalty'. Thus, the author becomes the participant in the direct market process of sale of his literary work. Therefore, there is a new kind of 'professional' independence within integrated and dominant market relations. New intermediaries like literary agencies have emerged in this developed phase.
42. R. Williams, op. cit., p. 124.
43. Ibid., p. 125.
44. R. Williams (1975), *The Long Revolution*, Pelican, London, p. 300.
45. Ibid., p. 301.
46. Ibid., p. 304.
47. Williams rightly remarks: "The society is not a background against which the personal relationships are studied, nor are the individuals merely illustrations of aspects of the way of life. Every aspect of personal life is radically affected by the quality of the general life, yet the general life is seen at its most important in completely personal terms. We attend with our whole senses to every aspect of the general life, yet the centre of value is always in the individual human person not any one isolated person, but the

many persons who are the reality of the general life" (ibid., pp. 304–5).

48. Ibid., p. 306.
49. For instance, *Brave New World, Ni neteen Eighty Four, Fahrenheit 451* and all serious science fictions are formula social novels in which a pattern taken from contemporary society is materialised, as a whole, in another time or place. These resemble realistic novels: "Most of them contain, fundamentally, a conception of the relation between individuals and society; ordinarily a virtuous individual, or small personal group, against a vile society. The action, normally, is a release of tensions in this personal social complex ..." (ibid., p. 307). Raymond Williams observes further: "Our formula novels are lively, because they are about lively social feelings, but the obvious dimension they lack is that of a substantial society and correspondingly substantial persons. For the common life is an abstraction, and the personal lives are defined by their function in the formula" (ibid., pp. 307–8).
50. Ibid., p. 307.
51. Ibid.
52. Ibid., p. 312.
53. Ibid., p. 314. To Williams, this discovery is not rediscovery, as nostalgia and imitation are not only irrelevant but hindering; any new realism will be different from the tradition. The old naive realism is now dead as it depended on a theory of natural seeing that is not possible now. He rightly observes: "we now know that we literally create the world we see, and that this human creation – a discovery of how we can live in the material world we inhabit – a necessarily dynamic and active; the old static realism of the passive observer is merely a hardened convention ... art is more than perception, it is a particular kind of active response, and a part of all human communication. Reality, in our terms, is that which human beings make common, by work or language ... . Reality is continually established, by common effort, and art is one of the highest forms of this process. Yet the tension can be great, in the necessarily difficult struggle to establish reality, and many kinds of failure and breakdown are possible" (ibid., pp. 314–15).

54. A. Gramsci (1996), *Selections from the Prison Notebooks*, Orient Longman Ltd., Hyderabad, p. 12.
55. Ibid., p. 9.
56. See R. Selden, op. cit., p. 43.
57. Ibid.
58. Cited in R. Selden, op. cit., p. 44.
59. Ibid., p. 45.
60. R. Selden, op. cit., pp. 46–48.
61. Ibid., p. 48.
62. Milan Kundera (1986), *The Art of the Novel*, Rupa and Co., New Delhi.
63. Cited in Hans Bertens (1995), *The Idea of the Postmodern*, Routledge, London, p. 121.
64. See Manager Pandey, op. cit., pp. 133–44.
65. Herbert Marcuse (1970), *One-Dimensional Man*, Beacon Press, Boston.
66. Cited in R. Selden, op. cit., p. 34.
67. H. Bertens, op. cit., pp. 3–5.
68. Ibid., p. 5.
69. R. Selden, op. cit, p. 75.
70. R. Barthes (1977), *Image, Music, Text*, Hill and Wang, New York, p. 146. To Barthes, since different ideological principles can exist at the same time, "the ideological choice is not the essence of criticism nor 'truth' its ultimate test. Criticism is something other than making correct statements in the light of 'true' principles. It follows that the major sin in criticism is not to have an ideology but to keep quiet about it ... it is self-deception or bad faith" (R. Barthes (1972), 'Criticism as Language', in David Lodge (ed.), *Twentieth Century Literary Criticism*, Longman, London, pp. 648–49). Further, he says that a novelist or poet is supposed "to speak about objects and phenomena which, whether imaginary or not, are external and anterior to language. The world exists and the writer uses language; such is the definition of literature. The object of criticism is very different; it deals not with 'the world', but with the linguistic formulations made by others; it is a comment on a comment, a secondary language or meta-language ... applied to a primary language (or language-as-object). It follows that critical

activity must take two kinds of relationships into account: the relationship between the critical language and the language of the author under consideration and the relationship between the latter (language-as-object) and the world" (ibid., p. 649). It follows from the above that in Barthes' view, the task of criticism's meta-language is not to discover the forms of 'truth' but forms of 'validity'. "In itself, a language cannot be true or false; it is either valid or non-valid. It is valid when it consists of a coherent system of signs. The rules governing the language of literature are not concerned with the correspondence between that language and reality (whatever the claims made by schools of realism) but only with its being in line with the "system of signs that the author has decided on ..." (ibid.). Thus, he emphasises more on semiological aspects than sociological aspects. Hence, for him, the task of criticism is purely formal: "it does not consist in 'discovering' in the work or author under consideration something 'hidden' or 'profound' or 'secret' which has so far escaped notice (through what miracle? Are we more perceptive than our predecessors?) but only in fitting together ... the language of the day (existentialism, Marxism or psychoanalysis) and the language of that is the formal system of logical rules that he evolved in the conditions of his time ... critical writing, like logical writing, can never be other than tautology .... If there is such a thing as a critical proof, it lies not in the ability to *discover* the work under consideration but, on the contrary, to cover it as completely as possible with one's own language" (ibid., p. 650).

71. Ibid., p. 651.
72. See H. Bertens, op. cit.
73. Ibid., p. 10.
74. Cited in H. Bertens, op. cit., p. 47. Unlike Derrida, he does not equate speech and writing, and does not see both as marked by 'absence'. He finds oral speech suffused with presence, hence he promotes oral poetry and improvisations. According to him, the written language inevitably tends towards timelessness and metaphysics and must undermine itself through self-reflexibility, through the destruction of its representations that it offers. A spoken language has at least the potential of

speaking authentically. But he was marginalised in the arena of postmodernism due to his existentialist position.

75. Such language games can accommodate elements such as 'deontic statements prescribing what should be done ... with respect to kinship, the difference between the sexes, children, neighbours, foreigners, etc. Because of their narrative status, such 'language games' can have only limited social and historical validity or 'legitimation'. He further argues that such legitimations have lost their power due to internal erosion but he does not explain as to why the loss of transcendent legitimation should be so damaging to science. But his target is not the science itself or its transcendent status but the principle of 'transcendent' legitimation itself. To him, Habermas is not correct in identifying emancipation with an 'ultimate consensus'. For Lyotard, consensus is only "a particular state of discussion, not its end". However, he expects political emancipation to be realised through dissensus, not through Habermasian consensus. To Lyotard, consensus is the end of freedom and thought; on the other hand, dissensus allows us to have freedom and to think, i.e., to extend our possibilities. While for Habermas, emancipation follows a route that leads via temporary consensuses to an 'ultimate consensus', for Lyotard, emancipation depends on the perpetuation of dissensus, that is, on a permanent crisis in representation on an ever greater awareness of the contingent and localised – the unstable – nature of all norms for 'representing the world'. Like the deconstructionist avant-garde, Lyotard thus advocates a radical anti-representationalism. See Jean-Francois Lyotard (1984), *The Postmodern Condition: A Report on Knowledge*, University of Minnesota Press, Minneapolis, pp. 20–65.
76. H. Bertens, op. cit., p. 147.
77. Cited in H. Bertens, op. cit., p. 148.
78. H. Bertens, op. cit., p. 148. According to him, information turns into 'non-information' because of the media's binary structure of question and answer which pre-programmes all responses through polls, tests, games, etc. He says that whereas the real was produced, the 'hyper-real' was reproduced – it is a reproduced real, the real as the generation by models of a real without origin

or reality, constructed from miniaturised units, from matrices, memory banks and command models, a 'meticulous' reduplication of the real, preferably through another, reproductive medium. See J. Baudrillard (1988), *Selected Writings*, Mark Poster (ed.), Stanford University Press, Stanford, p. 144.

79. S. Best and D. Kellner (1991), *Postmodern Theory: Critical Interrogations*, Macmillan, London, p. 125.
80. See R. Selden, op. cit., pp. 84–86.
81. Ibid., p. 44.
82. F. Jameson (1983), 'Postmodernism and Consumer Society', in H. Foster (ed.), *The Anti-aesthetic: Essays in Postmodern Culture*, Bay Press, Washington, p. 112.
83. Ibid., p. 113.
84. Ibid., p. 114. Pastiche is a 'blank parody', a parody without parody's ulterior motive, without satirical impulse, without laughter, without that still latent feeling that there exists something normal compared to which what is being 'imitated is rather comic'.
85. Ibid., p. 125.
86. *New Left Review* (1984), 146, pp. 53–92.
87. Ibid., p. 64.
88. Cited in H. Bertens, op. cit., p. 170.
89. Edward Said (1989), 'Representing the Colonised', *Critical Inquiry*, Vol. 15, Winter, p. 217.
90. Ibid., p. 219.
91. Ibid., p. 225.
92. Cited in H. Bertens, op. cit., p. 31.
93. Cited in A. Swingewood, op. cit., p. 21.

5

The Structure of Hindi Novels

We have selected four Hindi novels *Rangbhumi* by Premchand, *Budhua ki Beti by* Pandey Bechan Sharma 'Ugra', *Dharti Dhan Na Apna* by Jagdish Chandra and *Parishishta* by Giriraj Kishor. For understanding the textual structure of these novels, an analysis is attempted in terms of the following:

(a) Time and place
(b) Characters
(c) Events
(d) Inner connections

Rangbhumi (by Premchand)

Time and Place

The story of the novel begins with the description of a village, namely, Pandepur, situated on the outskirts of Banaras (now Varanasi) city, in UP where there is no provision of streetlight, nor sanitation nor provision for drinking water. There are petty shops as well as houses of milkmen, drivers of horse/bullock carts and of labourers. The novel *Rangbhumi* begins with these words: "Town is the place where the rich people reside and do commercial activities. The land outside the town is a place for their entertainment and enjoyment. In the centre of the town there are schools for their children and also the courts which they use for the victimisation of the poor in the name of justice. The settlement of the poor is situated on the outskirts of the town."[1] The novel was written in 1925 when India was under the British rule and the masses had launched freedom struggle under the leadership of Mahatma Gandhi.

Characters

There are sixty-three characters in *Rangbhumi* as mentioned below: Surdas *(Chamar),* Ganesh, Bhairo *(Pasi),* Subhagi (wife of Bhairo), Bajrangi *(Ahir),* Jamuni (wife of Bajrangi), Dayagiri, Naikram *(Panda),* Jagdhar (*Bania*), Jhingur, Tahir Ali, Mahir Ali, Jahir Ali (three brothers), Kulsun (Tahir's wife), Rakia (mother of Jahir Ali), Jainab, Jahir, Jabir, Sabir, Nalima, Mithua (nephew of Surdas), Sais, Chunku (a village *Chamar*), Chaudhury (head of *Chamars*), Thakurdin, Vidyadhar (son of Thakurdin), Ghisu (son of Bajrangi), Shiv Sevak, John Sevak, Ishwar Sevak (father of John Sevak), Mrs John Sevak, Sophia (daughter of John Sevak), Prabhu Sevak (son of John Sevak), Mr Clark (Collector), Mr Senapati (predecessor of Mr Clark), Mr Hunter, F. Wilson (Barrister), Prof. Charles Simian (a social worker against drug-addiction), Mr Nilmani (general secretary of Kashi Railway Union), Mahendra Kumar (chieftain of Chatari Estate and Chairman of municipality), Kunwar Bharat Singh (father-in-law of Mahendra), Jahnawi (K. Bharat Singh's wife), Indu (Mahendra's wife and Bharat Singh's daughter), Vinay (son of Kunwar Bharat Singh), Prannath, Munim, Sardar Nilkanth Roy (Diwan of Jaswant Nagar), Indradutt (Vinay's friend), Daroga of jail, Daroga's mother, magician (from Hyderabad), Virpal Singh (an extremist in Jaswant Nagar), Munshi, Patwari, Officer, Dr Ganguli, (volunteer), Bhilni (mistri), Sohrabji (artist), Higan Singh (driver of Mahendra Singh), coachman, postman, John Bird, and Lord Bishop. In this novel, Surdas, an illiterate blind man from *Chamar* (dalit) community, is the central character. The profile of characters may be seen in the Table 1 below.

From the table, it emerges that in terms of number of characters, *Rangbhumi* is a big novel. Secondly, in terms of caste, it has the largest number of upper caste characters (20

Table 1

Profile of Characters in *Ranghbumi*

Caste	*Sex*	*Zamindar*	*Peasant*	*Labourer*	*Govt Service*	*Non-Govt Service*	*Traditional Workers*	*Others*	*Remarks*
1	*2*	*3*	*4*	*5*	*6*	*7*	*8*	*9*	*10*
(1) Scheduled Castes (dalit)	M	—	1	3	—	—	1	—	5
	F	—	—	—	—	—	—	3	3 (all domestic women)
(2) Backward Castes	M	—	2	1	1	3	4	—	11
	F	—	—	—	—	—	—	1	1 (domestic woman)
(3) Upper Castes	M	4	4	—	7	2	2	1	20
	F	—	—	—	—	—	—	3	3 (all domestic women)
(4) Muslims	M	—	—	—	1	1	—	3	5
	F	—	—	—	—	—	—	4	4 (all domestic women)
(5) Christians (Indian)	M	—	—	—	—	1	—	2	1 capitalist, 1 social worker, 1 old
	F	—	—	—	—	—	—	2	2 (one domestic, one social worker)
(6) Europeans	M	—	—	—	2	4	—	—	6
	F	—	—	—	—	—	—	—	—
Total	(M+F)	4	7	4	11	11	7	19	63

Source: Prepared by the author

males and 3 females), followed by the backward castes (11 males and 1 female) and scheduled castes (5 males and 3 females). This indicates a large space for the upper castes, small space for dalits and for backward class the space being in between. However, in terms of significance its central character is a dalit. Thirdly, in terms of gender, there are 50 male characters and only 13 female characters. This again shows larger space for males and small space for females. Fourthly, in terms of religion, the largest space is for Hindus (43 characters), followed by Christians (11 characters) and finally Muslims (only 9 characters). Finally, in terms of occupation, there are 4 *zamindars,* 7 peasants, 4 labourers, 11 government servants, 11 private service persons, 7 traditional workers and 19 others.

Events

Surdas used to sit for begging at a place by the side of the main pucca road linking the town. He was unmarried. First event occurred in the month of Kartik (October–November), when one John Sewak, his wife, son Prabhu Sewak and daughter Sophia Sewak visited this area. This family was a rich Christian family and in the course of their visit, they reached the spot where Surdas was sitting. They were in their motor car. Surdas followed them in order to get something. The family was not inclined to give any thing. However, Sophia was liberal and kindhearted and pleaded with her mother to give him a coin. Mrs Sewak had no coin and she did not like to give a rupee note. Actually, John Sewak had gone there with a desire to establish a cigarette factory in that locality. Subsequently, he came to know that part of the required lands (ten *bighas)* of the locality were owned by Surdas. Then he began to behave very politely with Surdas. Surdas, however, refused to sell the land because of its association with the memory of his ancestors. Further, he considered that village cattle would lose their grazing ground. Besides he was not prepared to take any decision in this regard without consulting the local people. John Sewak offered him a five-rupee note for his begging bowl, and five thousand rupees as price for his land. He refused both. John Sewak apologised for the disrespect shown by him to Surdas.

Everyday people of the settlement, belonging to different castes, used to recite 'bhajans' (devotional songs) in the temple of the locality. This activity depended chiefly on Surdas. He had a nephew, Mitthu, whom he loved very much. Mitthu's parents had died in his early childhood. Surdas used to take all the care for his upbringing.

In the meantime in reaction to the pressure exerted by Tahir Ali on Surdas for selling his land, his nephew Mitthu and another villager Bajrangi's (milkman) son Ghisu beat, Tahir Ali's children. Tahir Ali then beat Ghisu. Bajrangi then beat him badly with a stick and injured him. Tahir Ali complained to John Sewak who became angry as to why he was not careful. But subsequently he also complained about this incident to Mahendra Kumar by distorting the facts. He reported that the incident had taken place at the instance of Surdas, Bajrangi and his associates who entered the ladies' rooms and tried to tease and torture them. At this Mahendra Kumar became angry and promised him to help saying that being a democrat he was opposed to violence.

Second incident: Bhairo (belonging to *Pasi* caste, a dalit) beat his wife Subhagi because she had not washed the clothes of his mother. Subhagi left his house and went to Surdas who prevented Bhairo from beating her more. She started living in the hut of Surdas but Bhairo did not like her to stay in the house of one who was a Chamar (a different dalit caste); and, more important, who was blind. Bhairo said, "Now I will not keep that witch in my house. Such an insult by a Chamar !"[2]. He was of the view that had she eloped with a man of higher caste, or a rich person, then he would not have been so badly hurt. Consequently, Bhairo set Surdas's hut on fire at night and took away his money amounting to more than five hundred rupees. In fact, Surdas had kept this money for three purposes.[3] He wanted to go to Gaya on a pilgrimage for the salvation of his ancestors; secondly, he wanted to spend some money on the marriage of Mithua; and, finally, he wanted to construct a drinking well for the use of public. When a villager, Jagdhar, inquired from Bhairo about the incident, the latter admitted what he had done but Surdas did not talk of the theft of money because he felt that people would not like to accept the fact that a beggar had collected so much money. However, Subhagi took a firm decision to return to her husband's home and get the money back to Surdas who had lost his hut because of giving shelter to her. Mithua, finding the hut burnt, asked his uncle where they would live; Surdas replied that he would reconstruct it. Mithua then asked what would happen if somebody again set it on fire, Surdas replied that he would reconstruct it again. Again Mitthu asked what would happen if somebody set it on fire thousands and hundreds of lakhs of time, Surdas replied with a childlike simplicity: "Then we would reconstruct it hundreds of lakhs of time".[4] After a few days, Subhagi went to the house of Surdas and returned the money stolen by her husband Bhairo. At first he refused to take it back because it was a sin but at the insistence of Subhagi, he took it ultimately. But next day, Surdas returned this money to Bhairo and also revealed to him, at his request, that Subhagi had given this money to him. At this Bhairo beat her badly and deserted her and then she again took shelter in Surdas's house. At this, Bhairo complained to Mahendra Kumar, Chairman of the Municipality and Honorary Magistrate who fined Surdas and Subhagi (for ₹ 200 and ₹ 100 respectively) as Bhairo managed some outsider witnesses by greasing their palm because local witnesses did not agree to give false evidence against Surdas. However, Surdas was dissatisfied with the verdict of Mahendra Kumar and he openly requested the audience present in the Court compound as an appeal before the people in general: "I request all of you to tell me whether I am guilty in your eyes? Do you believe that I allured Subhagi and have kept her as my wife? If all of you believe so, then I sit on this ground and all of you should beat me with your legs. If I die by that beating, I would not be pained, as such a sinner deserves such a punishment. What would happen simply from this imprisonment? But if I am not guilty, then you please declare that I am not guilty. Then I would not feel sorry even for any kind of rigorous imprisonment".[5] At this, thousands of persons present on the site announced that Surdas was not guilty, rather the Court itself was dishonest. So, ultimately, the people collected subscription and paid the fine imposed on them. It was interesting that Prabhu Sevak, Jahnawi, Indu (wife of Mahendra Kumar) and others contributed to the fund for the fine. After release, Surdas came to know that somebody had set his hut on fire and Bhairo's shop was also burnt by somebody. Indradutt had collected subscription much more than fine. Therefore, the remaining amount was handed over by him to Surdas' but he did not want to make his hut out of this money rather he offered this amount to Bhairo for rebuilding his shop. At this Bhairo became disillusioned and after knowing the reality, he did not take money but begged him pardon. He also revealed then that he had stolen the money earlier from Surdas hut and had also set it on fire. At this, Surdas said: "It is our big mistake that we do not consider play as a play. If somebody wins by committing fraud, what will he gain? One should play in such a way that one's goal should be victory but he should not be disheartened by the defeat and he should not shirk from the path of honesty. One should not become so much over-confident following one victory that he would never get defeated in future. Thus victory and defeat go on together with the life".[6] Further, Surdas suggested Bhairo to build a new shop of wood, not of *tari* (toddy). Further, when second time Surdas got notice for acquisition of the remaining five *bighas* of land (earlier five *bighas* had been taken away), he again revolted because government did not pay market value of such lands and took all the lands forcibly. But when others insisted that he should take the proposed one thousand rupees (offered by the government) otherwise it would be deposited in the treasury, he declared this money to be used for social service to be done by the volunteers. The members of the settlement collectively started to construct the hut of Surdas without any payment. On the other hand, Tahir Ali came with Prabhu Sevak to settle his scores with them. Naik Ram, being in a drunken state and having the support of Mahendra Kumar challenged Prabhu Sevak saying that he would also deal with his Christianity. At this Prabhu Sevak became furious and started beating him badly and nobody came to his rescue. Later when the matter came to the knowledge of Surdas, he told Naik Ram not to think of taking revenge. However, as he got the news of this incident, John Sevak himself went to Naik Ram to apologise fearing that the latter would not only take revenge but also close the prospect of acquiring any land of the locality. Ultimately, Naik Ram was impressed by the politeness of Mr John Sevak and excused his son. However, Mrs Sevak did not trust these fellows and termed the Hindus in general as her enemies. Prabhu Sevak did not agree with her mother's views saying that white men had a difficulty in accepting Indian Christians as their brothers and in America white Christians did not mind oppressing black Christians. Therefore, he felt that the liberation of Indian Christians was possible only by Indians. John Sevak believed in having a good relationship with English officials so that they might become convinced of Indian Christians' loyalty to the state power. He was worried that Indian Christians had not entered the arena of politics, though they were advanced in education. Therefore, he wanted a separate identity of Indian Christians with special respect and privileges, otherwise they would be lost in the vast population of Hindustanis. Later, John Sewak approached Mahendra Kumar for convincing Surdas to give his land but he did not oblige him. Then he approached the District Collector, Mr Clark with whom Mrs Sevak wanted to marry her daughter, though Sophia did not like him.

Third event: Miss Sophia, daughter of Mr and Mrs John Sevak, did not like the behaviour of her parents, especially that of her mother, who was of rough tongue and narrow outlook. They often had a hot discussion regarding Christian religion and spirituality. Sophia had appreciation for Hindu families where different family members were free to hold different views about religion. One day Sophia while walking in the town, thought of going to the house of her school friend Indu. So she moved towards that place and saw a group of musicians singing songs of patriotism. Suddenly, fire broke out in a house having tiled roof and at the same time somebody began crying for fear of being drowned in a pond nearby. One person, who was carrying a bucket of water for extinguishing the fire, fell down and was about to be burnt in the fire. Sophia rushed to him and saved him. She also got partially burnt while helping that man. She then fell ill and was practically senseless for three days. She opened her eyes and found herself in the house of Kunwar Bharat Singh, the father of her friend, Indu. The man whom she saved was Vinay Singh, the son of Kunwar Bharat Singh, the local chieftain. Rani Jahnavi (wife of Kunwar Bharat Singh) told Sophia that it was just a rehearsal of the activity of Seva Samiti, organised by her son Vinay. This voluntary group worked at the time of disaster. Sophia, still in the state of illness, continued to stay in that house. She came to know from her friend, Indu, that her father (Kunwar Bharat Singh) was a very religious person (devoted to Lord Shiva), her mother never did any *pooja,* her brother Vinay was an atheist and she herself was a devotee of Lord Krishna. Sophia became very happy to find the coexistence of such diverse views of faith in the same family. Later Mrs John Sevak went to Kunwar Bharat Singh's house to bring Sophia back. She proposed that her mother should assure her that she would not interfere in her freedom of holding her own religious views. But her mother told her frankly that there was no space in her home for any critical view regarding Jesus Christ. Mrs Sevak also spent sometime with Mrs Kunwar Bharat Singh and the latter appreciated Sophia very much and criticised her own daughter, Indu, for not knowing even the annual income of her estate Chatari. Sophia chose to stay in that house. John Sevak somehow convinced Kunwar Bharat Singh about the merits of industrialisation and the prospects of his proposal of establishing his cigarette factory. Kunwar Bharat Singh decided to take shares of fifty thousand rupees in that factory when Mr John Sevak assured a good profit in that enterprise.

Fourth event: Vinay's adoption of simple lifestyle helped him transcend his class. Therefore, Sophia inclined to marry such a *yogi* because she found in him pure love that bordered on devotion. However, due to social sanctions, Vinay and Sophia did not meet each other though they were residing in different wings of the same palace. Meanwhile Rani Jahnavi got some indication of this and, therefore, sent her son Vinay to Rajputana for working in the interest of the nation. She did not allow any letters delivered directly to Sophia. One day she told Sophia frankly that she had sent her son to Rajputana in order to prevent the closeness between her and Vinay. She also told her that they could not marry each other because of the religious barrier. She also clarified that she wanted her son Vinay to work wholeheartedly for the country. Therefore, she requested her not to indulge in love with him. She also requested Sophia to write a letter to Vinay that there was only a relationship of brother and sister between them. Sophia assured her that she would do so.

Later, Mrs Sevak went to bring Sophia back and there she told Rani Jahnavi that Mr Clark wants to marry her, and she appreciated her own family for mixing with the English people. At this, Rani Jahnavi told her that mixing with English people was not a question of respect amongst Hindus and Muslims. Further, when Mrs Sevak praised the English people for introducing railway, wireless, ship and postal services, Kunwar Bharat Singh told her that these developments would have been done even without the English people. However, such things were introduced by the English people for their own interests. Further, when Mrs Sevak appreciated the new justice system, then Kunwar Bharat Singh again told her that the new justice system was only a deception where injustice was proved as justice and untruth was proved as truth. Thus, there were opposite views about the British rule.

Fifth incident: When the lands of Pandepur were acquired with the help of the administration including municipality, Mr Clark enquired from Mr John Sevak whether Surdas was paid compensation for his land or not. Mr John Sevak replied that he had refused to take compensation, hence his money had been deposited in the state treasury. Then a Christian barrister, who was a rival of Mr Mahendra Kumar, told Mr Clark that one could not be forced to take compensation for one's land unless it was proved that the land acquired was for public purpose. Similarly, an old rival of Mr

John Sevak, the owner of Kashi Iron Works, Mr John Bird, also criticised the opening of a cigarette factory. Third person, Prof. Charles Simian, who had been opposing cigarette smoking on health ground, observed that if government could give land for opening cigarette factory why could it not give land for establishing a brothel? Fourth person, Mr Nilmani, Secretary of Kashi Railway Union, observed that such *land* acquisition law was for the benefit of only the capitalists. Mr John Sevak then realised that it was very difficult to keep such persons silent, though he had managed it with other families of the settlement. Then Mahendra Kumar told John Sevak that he himself was criticised by the public for it, yet both of them went to Pandepur. Mahendra Kumar assured two types of help to the settlement – water supply and supply of lanterns for street lights. While most of the families did not object to the land acquisition, Subhagi suddenly went there and complained: "Injustice has been done to Surdas. If his prayer is not heard, he will die."[7] Further, when Mr John Sevak said that how could government be stopped from taking up new work due to fear of death of Surdas, Subhagi reacted strongly: "Sir, the duty of government is to support the subjects, not to uproot them. Since this land has been acquired, the poor Surdas has forgotten to eat and drink. He is the only support for poor women otherwise the males of the settlement would not have spared the women and all males have a conspiracy against women."[8]

Sixth event: Sophia planned another way to influence Mr Clark by displaying her love for him. Mr Clark told her that he thought that she would be happy due to land acquisition for her father's factory. Here again, Sophia felt humiliated because her view was different from that of her father. Ultimately, to please Sophia, Mr Clark revoked his permission of land acquisition, because it was not for public purpose but for private interest. Later Sophia met Surdas and asked him to take revenge against Mahendra Kumar. He replied that in a game two parties were not enemies, rather the winning team embraces the defeated team. On the victory of Surdas, while outsiders appreciated it, most of the families of the settlement became his rivals because they apprehended that Surdas might be thinking of them as mean. However, Thakurdin thought that Surdas must be having the blessings of some god. But Sophia became disillusioned with Mr Clark and remembered in her heart that Vinay was an ideal person. Actually she was attracted to Lord Krishna rather than Jesus Christ.

Seventh event: Mahendra Kumar, Dr Ganguli of Seva Samiti and some of the public and traders' associations petitioned to the Council and Governor regarding non-cooperation of the District Collector for the establishment of a factory by an Indian. On this ground, Mr Clark was transferred as Political Agent to Udaipur, which suited Sophia because she wanted to go there along with Mr Clark as Vinay Singh was imprisoned there. Then, Mr Clark and Sophia went to Udaipur and they made a programme to visit the jail of Udaipur. There, Sophia met Vinay and both of them found that they still loved each other. Ultimately, Mr Clark signed an order for Vinay's release on the condition that he would not come to Udaipur without permission. Then Vinay departed for Delhi, where Sophia promised to meet him within a week. However, Vinay did not agree to leave Udaipur on the basis of that release order because he thought that it would be against her mother's desire. Meanwhile Naik Ram was sent by Kunwar Bharat Singh and his wife to bring Vinay back. Naik Ram somehow managed the jail staff and was successful in taking out Vinay from jail. While they were moving in the town, they met a crowd gathered due to the crushing of a man by the motor car of Mr Clark and Sophia. Mr Clark had also fired at the crowd in which one person had died. When somebody threw a stone on Sophia, suddenly Vinay fired at the crowd in which another person was killed. Ultimately, Sophia and Vinay went to some tribal village and stayed there for one year and came back to Banaras (now Varanasi).

Eighth event: The effects of new cigarette factory were mostly negative though new petty shops were opened for factory workers. There were shops for *tari* and wine. Further, there emerged seats of gambling and brothel. Thus, youths became their customers and the morality was vitiated. One day Ghisu, son of Bajrangi, and Vidhyadhar, son of Thakurdin, entered the hut of Surdas with the intention of forcing Subhagi to satisfy them sexually. But she and Surdas cried loudly and caught hold of them. Then many persons gathered there. While most of the persons present there requested Surdas to excuse them, he did not agree and complained it to the Police Station and, therefore, they were imprisoned for three months.

Ninth event: John Sevak needed some more land for a housing colony for the factory workers and, therefore, the entire housing site of the settlement was also acquired. While others hesitatingly accepted the compensation, Surdas refused to take it. He declared that one could forcibly take over his hut but not on the ground of justice. He also told that he had the "strength of getting killed". The informal *Mukhiya* of the settlement, Naik Ram, became the middleman between the local people and the officials. The new Collector, Mr Senapati, in order to show his loyalty to the government, reduced the amount of compensation by half. But the people were determined to support Surdas. So because of not solving the problem Senapati was transferred and Mr Clark was again posted there as District Collector. Mahendra Kumar came to persuade Surdas to accept compensation and leave the hut, but Surdas talked of moral duty and justice "... the duty of Government is to support the subjects, not to uproot and damage them".[9] Surdas also talked of *dharma,* not the so-called rule of law made by the government. Then, there gathered a big crowd and Superintendent of Police and armed force came there to tackle the situation. The SP ordered for firing three rounds in which about one dozen persons were killed including Indradutt, the leader of the volunteers. After that, SP again ordered for firing but the Havaldar and constables refused to fire on the innocent people. The death of these agitationists was celebrated by the local people as a sign of martyrdom. Indu also participated in the celebration of the death ceremony. Next day, Mr Clark went to the spot where the hut of Surdas was existing like a 'stage' (Rangbhumi) of the drama and Surdas was standing there in front of his hut looking like the *Sutradhar* of the play to be staged. Mr Clark used his *hunter* (whip) but despite the use of force by the police, people made Surdas their hero and made him sit on their shoulders. Then Mr Clark fired on Surdas, who fell down. At this, there was a charged situation. Some persons saw Vinay who told that he had sympathy with the agitationists and it was a victory of truth. At this, some persons taunted him for being elitist and busy in his love affair with Sophia. At this Vinay became emotional and took out his pistol and then shot himself dead to convince them about his sincerity of purpose. Sophia became disturbed hearing the death of Vinay, but she did not lose her heart. Similarly, Vinay's mother Jahnawi remained very bold and appreciated Vinay for his courage. All of them went to meet Surdas in the hospital. Even Mahendra Kumar, John Sevak and Kunwar Bharat Singh also went to Surdas to apologise. He told them that the voice of conscience should be the guiding principle for any action. Before dying, Surdas called his nephew, Mitthu, and wanted his assurance for performing rituals for his salvation as he was the only member of his caste and family, However, he declined to do so because he had no money. But others assured him that his wish would be fulfilled. He also requested John Sevak to help Tahir Ali, whose children were in trouble due to his removal from service. Before his death Surdas stated in a state of semi-consciousness: "Stop, why do you beat me now when you have won and I am defeated. I could not play well so you were winner. You are a matured player and committed fraud and you have tremendous spirit. On the other hand, we have less spirit, we do not commit fraud with players, rather we fight amongst ourselves and nobody listens to others. You are skilled in playing but we are amateurs. This is the only difference. Why are you giving big hands? It is not the duty of the winners to do so; your duty is to pat us; if we are defeated, so what? We did not run away from the field, did not weep and did not commit any fraud. We will play again after some rest and learn from you how to play after being defeated frequently and one day we shall win certainly."[10] Then he died and after his death Mr Clark also repented for killing such a noble man. He also told that the British government was only afraid of such a person who rules over the hearts of the people. He also repented for killing such people whom he worshipped in England. Later, some people collected the subscription and got an idol of Surdas built up. Sophia and Indu also contributed to this endeavour. Mahendra Kumar was unhappy for Indu's contribution. Then Indu asserted her dignity and self-respect and told him that though she was married to him, she had not sold her soul. She left him and went to her parents' house. After the inauguration of the idol, Mahendra Kumar went there in the night and damaged it. But, while damaging it, the big idol fell on him and he died on the spot.

Tenth event: Sophia's mother, Mrs Sevak, wanted Sophia to marry Mr Clark. Sophia assured her to do so the next day. But, in the night, she jumped into the Ganga river and left a letter addressed to her mother that she could not live in that world without Vinay who was calling her from the heaven and her jumping into the river was her actual marriage with him. Consequently, Vinay's mother became more active by becoming a fulltime volunteer. Kunwar Bharat Singh became more attracted to his property and luxury. Thus, he became a *zamindar* – capitalist in the real sense. Simultaneously, the factory of John Sevak expanded very much and he was planning to open one more factory at Patna. But Indu decided to make a public trust to be headed by Dr Ganguli. Thus, Indu, her mother, Jahnavi, and Dr Ganguli joined together for rendering collective service to the nation but Kunwar Bharat Singh started living a luxurious life with all pomp and show of the rich class.[11] There the novel ends.

Inner Connections

Rangbhumi indirectly presents a scenario of national freedom struggle. Surdas and other villagers' struggle is not against industrialisation (economy) but against the colonial system (polity) whose manifest face is represented by Mr Clark, district collector (executive's power of land acquisition without consent of landowner), Honorary Magistrate Mahendra Kumar (Judiciary's one-sided justice system), etc. Similarly Vinay represents a nationalist freedom fighter of radical wing and goes to Rajputana, on his mother's direction. Sewa Samiti represents Indian National Congress and its volunteers go to Udaipur, Poona (Pune), Garhwal, Punjab, etc. Further, Surdas through his good qualities like his belief in non-violence, truth, helpfulness, women's emancipation, inner knowledge and justice represents Mahatma Gandhi. Surdas's qualities/worldview become manifest one by one as the story moves from one event to another. For instance, he gives shelter to Subhagi; he tells Bhairo that his wife had given him that money which he returned to Bhairo; he protests the judgment of fining him and Subhagi for wrong allegations; he protests non-violently against the land acquisition by force; he gives money saved from the public subscription to Bhairo for building of his shop rather than his own hut; he still loves his nephew despite his naughtiness. He considered traditional rituals (like *tarpan)* as means of integrating people with their history. Again, by depicting an illiterate and blind man from a dalit caste from rural area, the novelist wanted to inspire the illiterate masses to rise up to the occasion of national freedom struggle. Finally, Indu's decision of making a trust in the end of the novel indicates that Gandhi's concept of trusteeship is worth practising.

Budhua ki Beti (by Pandey Bechan Sharma 'Ugra')

Time and Place

The novel, *Budhua ki Beti,* was published in 1928 (when India was under British rule) and it was written by Pandey Bechan Sharma 'Ugra'.[12] Its story is located in the city of Banaras (now Varanasi), UP. The novel ends with the departure of one of the main characters (Radha), in the company of Mr Young, to London by a ship.

Table 2

Profile of Characters in *Budhua ki Beti*

Caste	*Sex*	*Zamindar*	*Peasant*	*Labourer*	*Govt service*	*Non-govt service*	*Traditional workers*	*Others*	*Remarks*
1	*2*	*3*	*4*	*5*	*6*	*7*	*8*	*9*	*10*
(1) Scheduled Castes	M	—	—	—	—	—	5	—	5 (traditional job of sweeping)
	F	—	—	—	—	—	4	—	4 (traditional job of sweeping)
(2) Backward Castes	M	—	—	—	—	1	2	—	3
	F	—	—	1	—	1	—	—	2
(3) Upper Castes	M	3	—	—	2	3	7	1	16
	F	—	—	—	—	—	—	1	1 (domestic woman)
(4) Muslims	M	1	—	—	—	—	2	—	3
	F	—	—	—	—	—	—	—	—
(5) Christians (Indian)	M	—	—	—	—	—	1	—	1
	F	—	—	—	—	—	—	—	—
(6) Europeans	M	—	—	—	1	1	—	—	2
	F	—	—	—	—	—	—	1	1 (social worker)
Total	(M +F)	4	—	1	3	6	21	3	38

Source: Prepared by the author

Characters

There are thirty-eight characters in this novel and these are as follows: Gulab Chand, Ghanshyam, Barkat Ullah, Budhua, Radha, Pandit, mother-in-law of Budhua, Doctor Vaidya, Bairam (father of Ghanshyam), Sukli (second wife of Budhua), Kriparam alias Aghori Manushyanand, wife of Kriparam, student of Kriparam, servant of Aughar *math,* Seth, Liaqat Hussain, Rahman, Bhangin (sweepress), Bholia, woman of Kabir Chaura, youth, Daroga, Police Jamadar, Father Johnson, Reverend Wright, Mr Young, District Judge, Mrs Young, Guru of Manushyanand, Panda, second *pandit,* messenger of Panda, Feku (sweeper), Naresh (young sweeper), sweeper of the village, old sweeper, Tamoli and Sadhu. However, central characters are Budhua, and Aghori Manushyanand. The profile of characters may be seen in the Table 2 from which it transpires that, in terms of number of characters, it is a big novel. Secondly, in terms of caste, there are maximum 17 characters from upper castes (16 males and 1 female), followed by 9 from dalits (5 males and 4 females), and lastly 5 characters from backward castes (3 males and 2 females). This indicates larger space for upper castes but in terms of significance the novelist has depicted two central characters, one from Brahman caste (Aghori) and other from dalit caste (Radha). Thirdly, in terms of religion, there are 31 characters from Hinduism, 4 from Christianity and only three from Islam. This again shows larger space for Hindus who are in majority in India. Fourthly, in terms of gender, there are 30 male characters and only 8 female characters, indicating more space for males in traditional India. Finally, in terms of occupation, there are 4 *zamindars,* 1 labourer, 3 government servants, 6 private service persons, 21 traditional workers (mostly scavengers) and 3 others. This indicates larger space for traditional jobs.

Events

First event begins with the appreciation of beauty of Radha alias Radhia, the daughter of Budhua, a sweeper by caste. She was extremely beautiful surpassing the beauty of princesses and fairies. The novel begins with a dialogue initiated by one character Gulab Chand, "Oh! don't you know Radhia?".[13] Then he told his friend Ghanshyam that Radha did cleaning (not latrine-cleaning) work at the house of Barkat-ullah in Banaras (now Varanasi). One day Barkat-ullah teased her. She became angry and said, "I am a servant at your house for doing sanitation work, not to surrender my chastity; do not dare to repeat it in future".[14] Then, Budhua's first wife died of diarrhoea because the doctors of upper castes did not treat her in time. One doctor did not treat her because she was a sweeper while another doctor refused to visit her because he had no money to pay him and, therefore, his wife died due to lack of treatment. Consequently, Budhua felt dejected but later engaged himself in hard work. Further, he got rid of the habit of taking drugs and wine. He used to remember the death of his wife due to his poverty and caste prejudice. As a reaction, Budhua stopped working at the houses of doctors and took a pledge that he would never work in the house of a doctor even if he had to clean the excreta of dogs.

Second event: One day a migrant sweepress came into his locality from Gorakhpur town. She had been deserted by her husband. Therefore, the local community arranged the marriage of that migrant woman, Sukali, with Budhua. At this decision, a community feast was given by Budhua and on this occasion the spirits and other gods of the community were worshipped.

Third event: Manushyanand was a Brahman teacher but his beautiful wife was not faithful to him and she had an illicit relationship with another person (a disciple of Baba). One day Baba caught them together in his bed in his house. He, instead of punishing them, gave all the ornaments, clothes, etc., to her and told her to leave the house. Later, he distributed all his property amongst the beggars and poor people and then left his house for good.

Fourth event: Manushyanand adopted *'aghor'* cult and became known as *Aghori Baba* who later became famous for his supernatural power. Once Sukali was missing and Budhua's daughter Radha had fallen ill due to weeping continuously for her mother. Budhua wanted to meet Aghori Baba but he was prevented by others from meeting him on the ground of his belonging to an untouchable caste. Somehow, Baba heard that Budhua was prevented from meeting him, so he became angry with the crowd and ordered to bring Budhua to him. Then he took Budhua's hands in his hands displaying his respect and closeness. He also took Radha in his lap and she immediately stopped weeping. Baba openly showed others that he did not believe in untouchability. Later he said that Budhua's wife had gone to one Liakat Hussain who pretended to give boon of bearing sons to women as she was not happy with the daughter, Radhia. Budhua, then, went to the house of Liakat Husain with a razor and attacked him and his associates. He injured Liakat as well as killed his one associate and his wife. Thus, he became accused of murder and attempt to murder. He confessed before the police that he had committed the murder and had also injured Liakat Hussain by chopping off his nose.

Fifth event: Aghori Baba was worried about the upbringing of Radha. He approached many Hindu and Muslim families in this regard but none of them was ready to accept her. So he ultimately handed over the poor Radha to the Church priest for her upbringing. Aghori Baba and the Church priest, Johnson, discussed many social and religious issues threadbare. Aghori Baba told him that Indians were living in slavery and there were six crores of people as untouchables in the eyes of Hindus of India while other twenty-five crores of people were slaves and untouchables in the eyes of the outside world. While caste Hindus hated six crores of untouchables, the entire world hated all other Indians. In some regards, Aghori Baba said that Christians were better than Hindus because they did not believe in untouchability but he also criticised Christians for converting Hindu untouchables into Christianity. Aghori Baba also accepted that amongst Hindus there were many castes and sub-castes, high and low, but he also criticised Christianity which had hypocrites. There, Mr Young, the district Judge, was also present. Aghori Baba asked the Church priest Mr

Johnson "not to baptise" Radha and "to hand her over to her father Budhua in due course".[15] Mr Young was very much impressed by Aghori Baba.

Sixth event: The European women had formed a Women's Liberation Supporting Committee under the leadership of Mrs Young, the wife of the district Judge, Mr Young, but they used to indulge in various kinds of illicit relationships in the name of women's freedom. One day Agpori Baba took Mr Young to a place where European women were holding this get-together. When Mr Young and Aghori Baba saw that Mrs Young and other women were engaged in love-affair with other males, Mr Young became very angry. Mrs Young and other women covered the eyes of all males present there and declared that they invited only those males who played with the European women and then they jointly danced. Later such couples went to different isolated places in the jungle. When Mrs Young embraced a stranger male and kissed him, the latter wanted to open his eyes to reciprocate. At this Mrs Young commented: "A male is attractive only when he is blind. You remain as you are. I do not like males with eyes".[16] Hearing this from a distance, Mr Young wanted to take out his pistol and kill her, but Aghori Baba restrained him and reminded him that being a Judge he should follow the rule of law. But Mr Young was so much disturbed that he became senseless for a while. Aghori Baba carried him on his back, along with his bike in one hand. When he came to his senses, he realised that his wife was not loyal to him. He cursed Aghori Baba for restraining him from killing her. Aghori Baba again restrained him when he lost his temper. He told Mr Young that the world was a stage and life was a drama where they were simply actors. He also consoled Mr Young by saying that, like him, he had also seen the vulgar aspects of his wife but he controlled himself. Then Mr Young wanted to know the story of Aghori Baba. Aghori Baba described his past and hearing this, he appreciated Baba for granting pardon to his wife and his disciple. Then Baba said that even the Bible of Christians had many instances of pardoning the enemies but Christians did not understand the significance of pardoning.

Seventh event: In the trial, the Judge, Mr Young, sentenced Budhua for life imprisonment. He also ordered to release the accused if his behaviour remained good in the jail. After twelve years, Budhua was released from jail. At the railway station, Aghori Baba received him as he had promised earlier. He embraced Budhua and they went to the church priest to take Radha back. They found her well-dressed, well-mannered and her accent of Hindi was anglicised. The church priest, Mr Johnson, allowed Radha to go with her father Budhua. At the advice of Aghori Baba, Mr Johnson employed them as servants and gave a piece of land to make a hut. Both Aghori Baba and Mr Johnson were of the view that police purposely made the poor and the untouchables criminals and they exploited them in different ways. Due to this fear, Mr Johnson gave employment to Radha and her father Budhua. Radha used to address Mr Johnson as 'papa' and Budhua as 'father'. Mr Johnson told Budhua that Radha was hard-working and truthful but at the same time she could not tolerate hypocrites. Radha loved good clothes and eatables and, therefore, Budhua had to be cautious. Aghori Baba also suggested that if the innocent untouchables were properly organised, a revolt could take place easily.

Eighth event: One day Gulab Chand encouraged Ghanshyam to chase Radha. Gulab Chand also told Ghanshyam that if they did not advance towards her, some other non-Hindus like Barkat would exploit a Hindu girl. So one day both of them went to Radha's house near Durga Kund where on a piece of land, given by the priest, Radha's father had made a hut. Radha had kept a dog 'Spy'. She was swinging (in the month of *Asadh)*. Ghanshyam and Gulab Chand went near her. Radha objected but they did not stop, then while swinging she pushed Ghanshyam with her shoes and Ghanshyam fell down. On the other hand, the dog chased Gulab Chand fiercely. Ghanshyam felt insulted due to the beating by Radha, especially before the public. He started abusing the low caste women. Gulab Chand persuaded him not to beat a woman in revenge. He also told Ghanshyam that in love affair there was no question of high and low. Later, on the advice of the priest, Radha went to both of them and gave his watch, letter and other things which were left over there. This rekindled attraction amongst Gulab Chand and Ghanshyam towards her again.

Ninth event: One day Aghori Baba mobilised some untouchables and convinced them that they were untouchables due to their carelessness as well as for not taking bath. Further, their illiteracy had also made them low in the eyes of the general public. Moreover, he suggested them to abdicate all kinds of bad habits of intoxication and quarrelling amongst themselves. In addition, he also advised them not to commit theft and not to have desire for other women of the *mohalla* and of own caste. Finally, young ones should be taught new skills.[17] One young man named Naresh told his community people that he was a disciple of Aghori Baba. He did not drink toddy and other items of intoxication. He had also taken a vow not to commit theft nor would he allow others to commit theft. Second Panchayat of sweepers was held in a big field of Alaipur where the crowd of one thousand dalits assembled. The crowd was much bigger than that of the first panchayat. It was led by Aghori Baba who had got about fifty high caste youth as staunch volunteers. They criticised the superstitions in public. They visited the huts of sweepers and other low castes regularly to listen to their problems and advised them to be clean. They also helped them both in cash and kind. With the passage of time, Budhua emerged as the leader of his community. Due to Aghori Baba, he gave up eating meat and smoking *bidi*. Budhua told the crowd that they should be clean physically. Some of the people present in the crowd told that due to caste-prejudice high caste people did not allow them to wear clothes. Further, Budhua advised them for forging unity of the community and clarified that upper castes were as much dependent on them as they were dependent on the former. Therefore, the upper caste people should be clearly told that the society moves with love and cooperation, not with fear, dominance and atrocity. Later Aghori Baba also arrived there with *khappar* and *chimta* in his hands and looked like Lord Shiva. One woman brought her grandson who was ill, allegedly due to the effect of an evil spirit. Aghori Baba diagnosed him and told her that the child was suffering from stomach problem and he promised to give some medicine for treatment next day. Further, an old sweeper went there and requested to give him such a medicine so that he should die soon. He spoke of his miseries, how he worked hard to clean latrines, committed theft and went to jail many times and became ill but could never get food regularly. Even his only son had been sent to jail due to the conspiracy of the police. Aghori Baba consoled him. He told the crowd that he had gone there to fight against police excesses against the sweepers, therefore he advised them to be united. He further told the old man that he would manage his food and clothes from the next day. Then he told them that only by launching a movement the problems of sweepers could be sorted out. He encouraged them to form an organisation, to elect two *Panches* and follow their orders. Further he advised them to abdicate wine and other kinds of intoxication, and to be clean and not to commit theft and not to abuse each other. He also advised them to get education. He told them that he would start a factory for the untouchables for their employment and open a school for their children as he had got donations from many donors. Most of the crowd promised to abide by his suggestions.

Consequently, the sweepers threatened to go on strike and refused to clean the latrines and demanded to enhance their wages, make arrangements for education of their children, and municipality; government and society as a whole should arrange for their huts and also to allow their entry into the temples. They demanded that being Hindu devotees as well as human beings, they should be allowed to enter the temples. Thus, their demands were economic, social as well as religious. When a Hindu priest was expressing his hatred and disregard towards the sweepers' demands, a youth argued that with the change of society people had to change their traditional views and methods. The priest counter-argued that in Banaras (Varanasi) – the city of religiosity and piousness of the world – even the founder of Arya Samaj, Dayanand Saraswati was defeated and his views could not be accepted by the people, so Baba Manushyanand Aghori would also fail ultimately.

Tenth event: One day, Ghanshyam went to meet Radha. She was going on foot to the priest's house, and, therefore, he offered her a seat on his horse cart. She agreed somehow and this was repeated for many days. Radha thought that Ghanshyam was a good man as well as rich and respectful. Therefore, she also developed a soft corner for him in her heart. One day, Ghanshyam took her to his garden and outer house in the cantonment area. There Ghanshyam kissed her. Then she used to devote more time to Ghanshyam. Ghanshyam impressed her with food, flowers, music system, etc. When he offered many priceless things as gifts, she refused to take them with her due to fear of her 'papa' and 'father' though she was very much inclined to have those articles. Ghanshyam had declared himself to be unmarried though actually he was married. Radha was also willing to marry him but the problem was that Ghanshyam was insisting that she would have to desert her 'father' and 'papa'; to this, she did not agree. One day when they were in the garden, it started raining. That day Ghanshyam managed her for nightstay there against her wishes. For three days, rain continued. Consequently, Radha decided that she would not go to her father or papa and instead would live with Ghanshyam. When Radha did not return to her house at Sigra, Budhua went to search for her at the bungalow of the priest but she was not there too. In the rain, he returned again and he got fever. He and the dog, 'Spy', did not eat that day.

Several weeks and months passed but Ghanshyam did not allow Radha to go back to her house. One day Ghanshyam told her that Kashi, being an orthodox city, would not accept their married life publicly. Therefore, he advised her that for six months he would get himself separated from his father and with a handsome amount of money he, along with Radha, would migrate to somewhere else and settle there. He also uttered that "girls are born for husbands, not for *fathers*".[18] Ghanshyam used to impress her by his sweet words and Radha could not resist his desire. On the other hand, Ghanshyam had declared at his ancestral home that he was disenchanted and disillusioned with the material world, therefore he liked to stay at an isolated place. His rich father thought that his son was reforming himself and his friends thought that he had bowed down before his father's orders. Though Radha was not married with him, she started playing the role of his wife. Actually, Ghanshyam wanted to enjoy most of things in minimum time.

Eleventh event: When for months together Radha did not return, Budhua became seriously ill and weak. Then Aghori Baba served him in various ways and got him recovered. Aghori Baba assured him that Radha would return but at an appropriate time because her stars were bad. He also encouraged Budhua for actively participating in the movement of untouchables' reforms because due to his absence sweepers' movement had got a setback. He suggested him that he would got his daughter Radha back if he struggled for his community. Therefore, Budhua got convinced and took a firm decision to lead his community's movement. The threat of strike did not have much effect on the elites of the society. A Kayasth gentleman beat one sweeper when he threatened to go on strike. Further, the association for the resurrection of dalits was also firm and one rich person donated one lakh rupees for the progress of dalits. Further, one Ashram for the untouchables was opened at Alaipur mohalla. There, about 500 huts were constructed for sweepers, one school was also opened for their children's education. Furthermore, sewing and weaving works were started for the youths. Christian carpenters and blacksmiths were brought to the Ashram and these were ex-untouchables. About two dozens of volunteers were also engaged for teaching. Consequently, one day under the leadership of Budhram Chaudhary (Budhua) all the sweepers of Banaras deserted the old houses and went to the Ashram as a symbol of protest and the next day they went on strike.

Twelfth event: After living for six months with Ghanshyam, Radha realised that his love had declined because Ghanshyam had started staying for longer time in the city. He started telling her of his 'limits' and he also told her that he had to do a lot for earning money. Later, he did not like to talk about marrying her and if Radha ever talked about marriage, he used to digress from the issue. One night, Ghanshyam did not return and, therefore, she did not take her dinner. At midnight some people came there carrying Ghanshyam, who was intoxicated with wine and was senseless. But in that crowd there was one woman also and she was also intoxicated. Then Gulab Chand saw Radha there and was wonderstruck. He approached Radha and wanted to make love by embracing and kissing her but Radha pushed him back and she started kicking him with her legs; then the gardeners and the servants took Gulab Chand away from there. However, the other woman laughed at Radha and uttered that Ghanshyam Babu had another woman as a keep in the red-light area. Then, that woman and other visitors went away. This made Radha very much upset. After the departure of that prostitute from the garden of Ghanshyam, Radha fell down and fainted. When she came to her senses, she realised that Ghanshyam was a habitual cheat of innocent women like her. She became disillusioned with the dual character of Ghanshyam. She also realised the wickedness of Gulab Chand who thought of her as a woman of no virtue. She also remembered how bold her father Budhua was when he murdered two persons who teased her mother. Then she started weeping bitterly. By then Ghanshyam, lying in another room, also got awakened. When Ghanshyam went to her room, she became angry and told him: "Get away from here. Bad smell of wine comes from your mouth and bad smell of adultery comes from your body".[19] When he tried to console her, she became furious and called him a cheat, liar, bootlegger and womaniser. At this, Ghanshyam also became angry and asked her, "Have I cheated you? Which bank did you bring in your purse that I have cheated? I drink, so what? I have other keeps also, so what?; what right do you have to criticise me?"[20] At this Radha reacted, "Right you are, what right I have to tell the truth as the poor people and the victims have no right to speak."[21] And Radha went out of that room.

Thirteenth event: The strike of sweepers entered fifteenth day and the entire city turned into a hell due to dirt and bad smell. In some *mohallas,* people died due to the spread of epidemics of diarrhoea. Especially the women, children and the diseased had problem regarding attending to the call of the nature. Superintendent of Police, Kotwal, Collector and Commissioner had also gone to the Ashram to request the strikers to join their duty. But people's protest was beyond government's control. By then a section of people was convinced with their demands and were willing to accept those, but the older generation of caste Hindus was determined not to yield, although a section of upper caste youth was also willing to allow their entry into the temples.

Fourteenth event: Mr Johnson told Aghori Baba that he had got a letter from London from Mr Wright revealing that Mr Young had resigned from his service after going back to Britain, had divorced his wife and had started a business. Being influenced by Aghori Baba, he had deserted worldly pleasures of life. Mr Young also wanted to donate all his property of millions to Radha. Being issueless, Mr Young wanted that Radha should be his heiress. On the other hand, Mrs Young went to France and cheated an owner of a laundry by working in partnership with him. She had formed a committee involving women and men from European countries who walked naked at specific places for fulfilling their carnal desires. Consequently, Mr Young had spiritually risen above beauty and wealth, respect and disrespect. He was ready even to visit Kashi to take Radha there.

Fifteenth event: For twenty days the strike of sweepers continued and Radha was missing for eight months. Budhua became seriously ill though he was very much required at that moment to lead the movement of sweepers. There was a marked change in the dress of sweepers as well as their haircut. They started taking bath regularly. Some of the sweepers were of the view that they should not do the same job of sanitation rather would do new jobs like weaving of chairs, etc. Meanwhile, the sweepers got offers from the municipality for enhancing their wages, providing school for their children and houses for them. But the sweepers were firm to get their demand of entry into temples accepted. Some of them also demanded that everybody should clean his own latrine and he should not impose his dirty work on others. Rather following the advice of Aghori Baba they were ready to migrate to other places and work as coolies. One day, Budhua's condition became very serious. He was uttering in semi-consciousness: "How many more sins I have to bear? Outraging of the chastity of Radha's mother? What is this, is he the murderer of Radha's mother and her rapist? Why these images are gazing at me? Oh! it is Naini jail and it is myself Budhua, prisoner no. 365. I am sleeping in the jail and seeing myself too, what kind of dream is it? Radhia, I have gone mad, where are you? Please call my Guru Aghori Baba ... where did you go away by deserting me, the helpless."[22] He further uttered many things in introspection as to how he committed sins in the jail in order to see his daughter. Then Budhua started weeping bitterly. Aghori Baba was also moved and put his one hand on Budhua's body. Then Budhua became silent. At the instance of Aghori Baba, someone poured some water in Budhua's mouth. His desire before salvation was to see Radha. Further he also desired to enter Vishwanath temple at Kashi. Aghori Baba replied that his desires would be fulfilled.

Next day, there was a big demonstration of the sweepers. Many of the common people, who were opposed to sweepers' entry into the temple, were very much impressed by Aghori Baba and his blessings. A big crowd went to Ganga river and took bath and went towards the temple singing and chanting slogans. There was one view amongst the common people that if the strike of the sweepers continued only due to the unyielding stand of the Brahmans and priests, many citizens of the town would support sweepers' entry into the temple. As one them was of the view that at some temples even dogs had a free entry, then, why not sweepers be allowed inside. Then the demonstrators with enthusiasm passed through the town under the leadership of the Aghori Baba and Budhua. The traditional priests became afraid of the angry volunteers and sweepers, especially Budhua who was moving in a palanquin on the shoulders of the crowd looking like a god. Nobody dared to oppose their entry into the temple, the big crowd suddenly entered the temple. After the departure of the crowd, the traditional priest got the temple duly washed and worshipping rites were conducted. Finally, an agreement between the sweepers and the municipality was executed, especially in terms of doubly enhancing the wages, building of houses, opening of schools for children and for upgrading skills of adults, construction of a new temple by social reformers for the dalits and their entry into other temples.

Sixteenth event: Radha left the garden and the outer house of Ghanshyam. After walking some yards, she stopped under a tree and again thought of the wickedness of Ghanshyam. After sometime, 'Spy' dog came over there. Once she thought to commit suicide but due to the polite and loyal behaviour of her dog, she went towards her father's house. However, on the way, she found one person, who was blind and his nose was chopped off, crying. He was restless and praying God to award him death. He was also uttering about his wickedness of cheating others and being in jail for four years. Hearing his weeping, Radha approached him and consoled him. She promised to serve him regularly there.

Seventeenth event: One day, Aghori Baba followed the dog 'Spy' and they reached an abandoned house where Radha was serving a beggar for months. Aghori Baba brought Radha and that beggar, Liakat Hussain, who had outraged the modesty of Radha's mother and whose nose was chopped off by Budhua, also into the Ashram. Seeing Radha, Budhua finally got the awaited salvation. There Aghori Baba, Mr Johnson and two Europeans were also present among the crowd. Radha was weeping at her father's death.

Eighteenth event: Mr Young took Radha to Britain as his heiress. The priest Johnson and Aghori Baba duly bid adieu to

Mr Young and Radha. The novel ends with the departure of Radha and Mr Young by ship from the Bombay (now Mumbai) port.

Inner Connections

The Hindu hierarchical order with its salient feature of exclusion is directly challenged here in order to make it into horizontal order characterised by inclusion. This was thought necessary in view of the emerging trend of conversion of dalits into Christianity that has no apparent system of untouchability. That is why Aghori Baba appreciates Christianity's egalitarian aspect but criticises its new tendency of conversion of dalits. In the novelist's view, if dalits are provided due space with dignity within the Hindu social order, especially Aghor Panth, the threat of conversion would vanish automatically. That is why the novelist allows the entry of dalits in the sanctum sanctorum of Vishwanath temple, one of the highest citadels of Hindu religious power in India. Further it transpires that the novelist chose Aghori, not a *Vaishnava,* nor a *Shaiva,* nor a *Nanakpanthi,* etc., because Aghori is related to *tantra* cult, belonging to Lokayata school of Indian philosophy in ancient days. In this tradition there is no consideration of *jati/varna.* It is directed against the caste order of society and values only the individual's merit and virtue.

Dharti Dhan Na Apna (by Jagdish Chandra)

Time and Place

The Hindi novel *Dharti Dhan Na Apna,* written by Jagdish Chandra, was first published in 1972.[23] This novel is based on his memories of his mother's parents' village, Ralhan, in Punjab.[24] The author used to visit the Harijan settlement there as one Harijan (Chamar) family cultivated the lands of his mother's parents. He was a student of economics and, therefore, observed the economic exploitation of the Harijans very closely. He has written in the Preface of the novel that he found the Harijans under feudal exploitation for quite a long time. Though he does not belong to the Harijan community and, therefore, did not have direct experience of the Harijans, yet he has closely and empathetically observed their plight. He also claims that he has not used his own opinion or ideology in the depiction of characters in this novel.[25]

Characters

In this novel there are fifty-one characters as follows: Kali, his aunt, Pratapi, Nikku, his wife, Prito, daughter Lachho, his sons, Amaru, Jitu, Prasinni, Tai Nihali, and Nand Singh, his daughter, Pasho, Chaudhari of Chaubare, Chaudhuri Harnam Singh and Chaudhurain, his nephew, Hardeo, Santu, Mangu, domestic servant of Harnam Singh, Jasso, mother of Mangu, Gyano, sister of Mangu, Bebe Hukuma, Chhajju Shah, Kumbhkar, Babe Phatte, Bagga, Ghumman, Fauja Singh, Dinu, Santa Singh, Nattha Singh, Khusia, Lallu Pahalwan, Dilsukh, Balwanta, Dr Vishandas, Ome, Munshi, Church priest, his wife, temple priest, Buta Singh, Basanta, Tirathram, Jagta, Chaudhuri Palo, Bela Singh, Rakhe Dhewar, Acharya Rudluram, Tahal Singh and Channa Singh. In this novel, Kali is the central character.

The profile of characters may be seen in Table 3. It transpires from the Table that in terms of number of characters, it is a big novel (51 characters). Secondly, in terms of caste, dalits have the largest number (27), followed by backwards (13) and lastly, very few upper caste characters (2). This shows larger space for dalits numerically. Further, in terms of significance too, the central character of the novel is a dalit, Kali. Thirdly, in terms of religion, there are 42 characters from Hinduism, 7 characters from Sikhism, and only 2 characters from Christianity. This shows larger space for Hindus who have a majority in India. Fourthly, in terms of gender, there are 40 male characters and only 11 female characters, indicating larger space for males. Finally, in terms of occupation, there are 3 *zamindars,* 11 peasants, 25 agricultural labourers, 1 government servant, 4 private service persons, 6 traditional workers and 1 other worker.

Table 3

Profile of Characters in *Dharati Dhan Na Apna*

Caste	*Sex*	*Zamindar*	*Peasant*	*Labourer*	*Govt service*	*Non-govt service*	*Traditional workers*	*Others*	*Remarks*
1	*2*	*3*	*4*	*5*	*6*	*7*	*8*	*9*	*10*
(1) Scheduled Castes	M	—	—	15	—	—	2	—	17
	F	—	—	10	—	—	—	—	10
(2) Backward Castes	M	3	5	—	1	2	2	—	13
	F	—	—	—	—	—	—	—	—
(3) Upper Castes	M	—	—	—	—	1	1	—	2
	F	—	—	—	—	—	—	—	—
(4) Sikhs	M	—	6	—	—	1	—	—	7
	F	—	—	—	—	—	—	—	—
(5) Christians	M	—	—	—	—	—	1	—	1
	F	—	—	—	—	—	—	1	1 (domestic woman)
Total	(M+F)	3	11	25	1	4	6	1	51

Source: Prepared by the author

Events

The *first event* of the novel begins with the return of Kali from a town where he was working for years: "When Kali reached the village it was an early dawn ... he took off his trunk from his head and the bedding from his shoulders and kept these on the ground. Sitting on the roots of a tree, he thought that in the field of Choudhary Fattu, his son, Pyaru, might be ploughing ...".[26] Kali passed through the old school of the village (where he had studied) after crossing the settlement of Chaudharis (Jats). He reached the village temple, passed through the settlement of shopkeepers and then he saw the church. When he proceeded ahead, he got a bad smell of cow dung and that was the beginning of 'Chamadari' (Chamar's or Harijans' settlement). When he reached his home, he found his aunt Pratapi ill. He had lost his parents in his early childhood and had been brought up by his widow aunt who was the only member in the family. Kali had fled away from his native place about six years ago. Next day he discovered that new *bundhs* had been constructed outside the village. He also found one Jat farmer, Chaudhari Harnam Singh, abusing and beating one Chamar labourer, Santu, and then another Chamar labourer, Jitu, without confirming as to who was responsible for grazing of maize crop in his fields. But none of the villagers openly protested against Harnam's conduct. Due to hitting with shoes, blood came out of the mouth and nose of Jitu. Only then was the beating stopped. Most of the Chamar labourers were of the view that they could not face the Chaudharis. Some Chamars, especially Mangu, the bonded labourer of Harnam Singh, were happy with the beating of Jitu. Mangu used to be instrumental in such kinds of exploitation of the Chamar labourers in order to show his loyalty to his boss. A woman named Prito did condemn Jitu due to her family's closeness to Mangu. In fact, Mangu used to sexually exploit Prito and her daughter and, in return, used to give some food, etc, to this starving family.[27] It is very interesting that when Gyano (sister of Mangu) came to know that Harnam Singh had badly beaten Jitu, she started abusing him (Harnam), but her mother Jasso immediately stopped her by reminding her of dire consequences. The village shopkeeper, Chhajju Shah, requested the aged Chamars to persuade their young members not to damage the crops and he also requested Harnam Singh to excuse them. When Chhajju Shah asked as to whether, Kali would stay in the village permanently or just temporarily Kali in reaction replied that he desired to go back to the town by the night train. Before Kali's departure, Choudhari Harnam Singh threatened all the Chamars collectively that if anybody damaged his crops, he would get the entire Chamadari beaten up. Hearing this, Kali felt as if this threat had been directed towards him. Therefore, his gazed protestingly at Chaudhari Harnam Singh, who felt bad but continued to threaten.

Second, the reaction of the Chamars to the exploiter's beating of Jitu was of four types:

(a) Pro-active reaction to take revenge with the exploiter – rarest of the rare (for example, Kali);
(b) Semi-active reaction in the form of abuses for the exploiter in his absence (e.g., Gyano);
(c) Passive reaction in the form of cursing the exploiter (e.g., Bebe Hukma, Nihali).
(d) Negative reaction in the form of finding faults with the victim (e.g., Mangu, Prito).

Third, when Kali went to the shop of Chhajju Shah next day, the latter offered him a cigarette and told him boldly that Jitu was unnecessarily beaten up for no fault of his because on that very day he was busy in doing the work of the shopkeeper till late night. Then Kali shared his intention of constructing a *pucca h*ouse in place of his old thatched roof. The shopkeeper realised that Kali had earned enough money and, therefore, he again offered him one more cigarette. When Kali told him that he does not like cigarette much, rather he would prefer *hucca* (tobacco pipe), the shopkeeper replied that he had two extra *huccas,* one for Jats and the other for Chamars, but a few days back one Chamar customer used that hucca and took that away with him. Thus, the shopkeeper indirectly refused to share his own *hucca* with Kali. Further the shopkeeper, who was also working as moneylender, told Kali that his

(Kali's) uncle Siddhu had taken a loan of ₹ 100 for the construction of house twelve years back and still a sum of twenty-five rupees was due from him. Next day, Kali paid that amount, but then the moneylender-shopkeeper asked for twelve rupees more as interest. Even that was paid by Kali, though with protest.[28]

Fourth, when Kali started to construct his pucca house, Mangu raised an objection that Kali could not use the silt and soil of the village pond without the permission of Harnam Singh. Kali did not accept Mangu's terms. The latter started abusing and quarrelling with him and, therefore, Kali beat him up badly. The matter was reported by Mangu to Harnam Singh in a distorted way. However, when Kali clarified the entire episode to Harnam Singh, the matter was resolved. Later, Mangu conspired with Kali's neighbourers, Prito and her husband Nikku, for not allowing him to construct his house without getting the land measured. However, following the official measurement, it was found that Kali's land was wrongly encroached by his neighbour. Even for this routine task the local government employee and one village middleman, from Jat caste, took bribe from Kali.

Fifth, when Kali went to the *rajmistry* (mason), Santa Singh, a Sikh, he commented on the quarrel of Kali and Nikku in a very disgraceful manner: "In the village, it is very difficult to recognise the dogs and Chamars".[29] When Kali reacted to the comparison of Chamars with dogs, then Santa Singh said that it was just a joke. He told Kali that wherever he worked, he took lunch and evening tea at the house of the host but he could not eat and drink in Kali's house, so he demanded extra charges for that.

Sixth, when Kali had a shortage of money for house construction, he approached the moneylender-shopkeeper, but he refused on the ground that Kali had nothing to mortgage as a collateral. When Kali offered his house site, the moneylender told him that it was a common land that could not be transferred or mortgaged. It was only for the use of the Chamars. When he approached the church priest, he also did not help. When he approached the

Communist Party leader and a local quack, Bishan Das, he also refused to help.

Seventh, while playing *Kabaddi,* Kali caught hold of Hardev Singh, the nephew of Harnam Singh, the latter deliberately gave a strong punch on the chest of Kali and hurt him. However, a wrestler, named Lalu Pahalwan, treated him although he belonged to the Jat community.

Eighth, when one day Santa Singh was working on the house construction of Kali and felt thirsty, Kali offered his service to bring water from the house of Nand Singh, another Sikh converted from Chamar. At this Santa Singh reacted by abusing Nand Singh that the latter was only a Ramdasia Sikh (a convert from Chamar), and despite the change of religion caste did not change. Hence, he refused to take water from Nand Singh's house.

Ninth, when the postman brought a money order for Kali (his wages earned in the town earlier and sent by his employer), the postman told him that in future Kali should also write his father's name or caste or both in his address so that there was no confusion. Later, when the postman wanted some commission for delivery of money order, Kali refused and told him that the money order charges were already paid by the sender. However, Kali finally offered some coins to him as a dole; the postman did not accept it, but reacted strongly, that he was not a beggar and if at all he would be compelled to beg, he would beg from some trader or Chaudhari, but not from a Chamar.

Tenth, when Nand Singh realised that, despite being converted to Sikhism, his identity was still that of a Chamar, he approached the church priest for getting converted to Christianity. However, the Communist leader, Bishan Das, was of the view that class character of Nand Singh would not change despite his conversion to Christianity. He found out that the real cause of conversion of Nand Singh was securing a government job to his elder son in the town with the influence of the church priest. In the conversion ceremony, Nand Singh's family members were given new clothes, shoes, food, etc. However, other Chamars were not happy with their conversion.

Eleventh, Kali's aunt became very ill and despite the medical treatment, she did not recover. When, on the advice of the local doctor, Kali wanted to purchase milk, one Jat farmer Hari Singh refused to sell milk to Kali because he was a Chamar. Thus, Kali realised that in the town one could purchase anything with money but in the village either it was given free of cost or it was not given at all. Then he approached the church priest for milk and he gave him condensed milk. However, when his aunt did not recover from the medical treatment, on the advice of the village women, he called a local sorcerer to remove the ills using witchcraft. He also took money in the ritual but his aunt did not recover. The next day she died. Kali had to spend some money on the rituals of the death ceremony. Regarding arrangement for sitting of the community members for the death ceremony, he went to the church priest for help. The priest told that his own grandfather was a Hindu and when he had died, his family incurred a heavy expenditure in death ceremony and, therefore, his father, disgusted with that situation, joined Christianity. The priest, however, helped him by mediating with the new convert Nand Singh (alias Masih) to offer his hall. Kali found that the family of Nand Singh was practising new manners and customs of keeping loaves in a plate and even wearing shoes in the kitchen by imitating the Christians. However, Nand Singh continued to use *hucca* on the ground that once he left Sikhism there was no harm in using *hucca* again.[30] It was very surprising that on the day of the final death ceremony, Kali found that his money was stolen from his trunk. But unfortunately some of the women whispered that Kali might have deliberately hidden his money somewhere else and wanted to accuse others for theft. Hearing this, Kali wept bitterly because his aunt had died, further his money was stolen, he was also accused of theft and also some community members were angry with him.

Twelfth, Kali had no other member in his family to live with in his village house, so, instead of going back to the town, he started a petty task of cutting grass and selling to the shopkeeper and others for their cattle's fodder. One day when Kali was talking to Nand Singh, who told him that after becoming a Christian he was no more a Chamar, suddenly one village farmer Chaudhari Munshi addressed Nand Singh as Chamar while asking him for giving new shoes. At this, Nand Singh objected, then Chaudhari Munshi abused him and tried to assault him. Kali pushed Chaudhari Munshi aside and told him that Nand Singh was just demanding the price before handing over the new shoes. But Chaudhari Munshi assaulted Nand Singh physically, then again Kali caught hold of Chaudhari Munshi. Consequently, Chaudhari Munshi caught hold of Kali's collar and in that quarrel his clothes were torn. Meanwhile Chaudhari Harnam Singh also reached there. When Kali told the actual story of quarrel, Chaudhari Harnam Singh became angry and warned Kali that in any dispute between Chaudhari and Chamar, it was always the latter at fault. Kali was also reprimanded by some of his own community members like Basanta. On this incident, Mangu and Prito were happy whereas other community members were unhappy.

Thirteenth, during the rainy season, there came a heavy flood which threatened to wash away the entire village. When the community well of Chamadari sunk in the rainwater, there arose a problem of drinking water. When the Chamar women went to the temple well to take water, the temple priest objected and did not allow them to take water. Later, when they went to the church to take water from the hand-pump, the wife of priest became angry due to the dirt and filth created by those women, especially when one infant defecated near the hand-pump. Ultimately finding no better alternative, the Chamar women used rainwater for drinking.

Fourteenth, due to the sufferings from the heavy floods, the villagers collected subscription from the entire village and got one goat to sacrifice but even after that sacrifice, the fury of the flood did not stop. Hence, the villagers planned to break the *bundh* for which Kali and Harnam's nephew Hardev jointly took risky initiative. Chamar labourers, who worked labouriously for removing the floodwater, did not ask for any wages from anybody because it was a collective work for the common interests of the entire village. But when the floodwater threatened to damage the crops of the Jat farmers, the latter wanted the Chamar labourers to work further to ensure fast flow of the floodwater from their fields. The labourers demanded wages from the Jat farmers but they refused to pay them. At this, Lalu Pahalwan (himself a Jat farmer) suggested that every Jat farmer should pay wages in cash or kind to his attached labourers. But most of the Jats did not agree to this proposal. When Harnam Singh abusingly tried to get work done without paying wages, Kali left the site along with his basket in protest. Therefore, other Chamar labourers also followed him.

Fifteenth, on the refusal to work without wages, the Jat farmers decided collectively not to allow Chamars to enter their fields for any work or private purposes like attending the call of nature. Then, Chamars responded this boycott by refusing to work under Jat farmers. While the local quack and Communist leader, Bishan Das, appreciated this protest by the Chamar labourers declaring it as a class struggle, he did not help them in giving them foodgrains to eat or any cash to purchase foodgrains from the market on the plea that contradictions should increase. Further, the village shopkeeper also did not give them foodgrains on credit on the plea that Jats would be angry. Moreover, the moderate Jat farmer, Lalu Pahalwan, also did not help Kali in giving foodgrains, on the plea that it was a matter of caste fraternity. Further, even the church priest also did not give them foodgrains on the pretext that he could not help non-Christians in this way. However, the Chamar women and men, who used to quarrel for petty things amongst themselves earlier, felt collective solidarity and mutual help necessary during the boycott.

Sixteenth, after about a week, the farmers could not continue to work in the fields and carry the headloads themselves. Further, the shopkeeper's business was also badly affected as most of his customers were Chamars but now they had no purchasing power. Then, the children of the farmers had to work in the fields and thus their education was also affected. Ultimately, the middle course of action, proposed by Lalu Pahalwan, was agreed: Chamar labourers should be paid the wages for one and half days. Then the labourers agreed to work under Jat farmers and the Chamar women went to the farmers households for domestic work. Thus, the struggle was mutually resolved within a week.

Seventeenth, after the death of his aunt, Gyano used to give Kaii some loaves to eat without the knowledge of her brother (Mangu) and mother. She used to visit his house and the fields at night also and this love affair slowly came to be known to the people of the locality, especially the young ones and women. Ultimately she became pregnant and she disclosed this secret to Kali who wanted to elope with her to the town but wanted some time to manage things. Meanwhile, after knowing the awkward situation, Mangu beat up his sister Gyano as well as Kali very badly. Kali also lost his temporary employment under Lalu Pahalwan. Her mother told Mangu about the pregnancy of Gyano. Both of them became very angry at it and felt helpless because any marriage with the village person of the same 'gotra' (clan) and being pregnant before marriage were against their prestige in the community and locality. Meanwhile, Kali went to the church priest to get converted to Christianity in order to marry Gyano but when the priest came to know that Gyano was underaged, he refused to help him in this regard. Further, the mother and brother of Gyano arranged *sankhia* (poison) and it was given to Gyano under the pretext of treating her stomach pain. Consequently, she died within a few minutes. Mangu also became very angry and wanted to take revenge with Kali but his mother prevented him by saying that she would take revenge herself and would not allow him to be alive in the village any more. Then, in the early morning after cleaning the vomited filth of Gyano, mother started weeping bitterly at the death of her daughter Gyano as if she had died naturally and all of a sudden. Here ends the novel.

Inner Connections

Dharti Dhan Na Apna is a novel based on the multidimensional reality of a village. The undercurrent of the novel is that the village is still bound by the traditional social customs of dominance over dalits and the real cause of such subordination is their lack of ownership of land. Hence, the existing exploitative pattern of landholding by the upper and middle castes on the one hand and cultivation by the landless dalits, on the other, is to be removed through a radical land reform. Secondly, church priest had been preaching to help the poor but he did not do so at the time of their struggle. Further, he does not solemnise the marriage of Kali and Gyano even though they were willing to embrace Christianity. Thirdly, Sikh mistry, Santa Singh, does not take water from a convert Sikh, because, in his view, caste does not change despite the change of religion. Finally, Communist leaders like Bishan Das and Tahal Singh do not help the struggling Chamars in terms of cash or kind because their ideology preaches that contradictions should get intensified more and more.

Parishishta (by Giriraj Kishor)

Time and Place

The novel *Parishishta* was written by Giriraj Kishor in early 1980s and was published for the first time in 1984.[31] Its location extends from rural area to a town in western Uttar Pradesh and then to Delhi.

Characters

There are forty-six characters in this novel. The novel begins with this statement about the central character, Anukul: "Anukul's (Ram's) story is as distasteful as Anukul (Ram) himself. Neither there is joy nor grandeur, absolutely cold. This is not simply his story but also the story of all the people who are attached with him ... . Only shaking shadows and shadows are visible but not a single face."[32] The characters in the novel are: Anukul, his father, Bawan Ram, his mother,

Table 4

Profile of Characters in *Parishishta*

Caste	*Sex*	*Zamindar*	*Peasant*	*Labourer*	*Govt service*	*Non-govt service*	*Traditional workers*	*Others*	*Remarks*
1	*2*	*3*	*4*	*5*	*6*	*7*	*8*	*9*	*10*
(1) Scheduled Castes	M	—	1	1	3	—	—	5	10
	F	—	—	—	—	—	—	5	5 (all domestic women)
(2) Backward Castes	M	—	2	—	2	1	1	1	7 (one MP)
	F	—	—	—	—	—	—	1	1 (domestic woman)
(3) Upper Castes	M	—	1	—	11	—	1	9	22 (one MP, 7 students)
	F	—	—	—	—	—	—	1	1 (student)
Total	(M+F)	—	4	1	16	1	2	22	46

Source: Prepared by the author

Parvati, an engineer, a foreman, Bawan's son-in-law, a dalit lady, a dalit child, Mr Chaudhuri (MP), his wife, his servant, Rajendra Singh (MP), Ram Ujagir, his father, Suvaran Chaudhuri, his mother, his aunt, his sister-in-law, his sister, Mohan, Baburam, Neelamma, Prof. Rao, Mr Khanna, Chanchal, Dinesh, Prof. Malkani, Prof. Athawale, Director, Dean, Warden, bus conductor, *masterji,* Kallu (constable), *daroga* (sub-inspector of police), Pandaji, Khajan Singh (driver), *scooterwala,* a *seth,* a doctor, Raju, Rajiv, Ravi (three students), Khalasi, station master, Harcharan and Kisan. Anukul is the central character of this novel. The profile of characters may be seen in Table 4.

From the above, it transpires that in terms of number of characters, it is a big novel (46 characters). Secondly, in terms of caste, there are 23 characters from upper castes, followed by 15 characters from dalits and only 8 from backward. This indicates larger space for upper castes. But, in terms of significance, here a dalit is the central character. Thirdly, in terms of religion, there is depiction of characters only from Hinduism. This shows a novel centred on one religion in a multireligion society. Fourthly, in terms of gender, there are 39 male characters and only 7 female characters. This indicates the larger space for males in traditional North Indian society. Finally, in terms of occupation, there are 4 peasants, 1 labourer, 16 government servants, 1 private service person, 2 traditional workers and 22 others. This shows larger space for government service

Events

First, when Anukul was born after two daughters, Bawan Ram got promotion to the post of Supervisor in that factory and since then he started thinking of his son's birth as a good omen. Therefore, he gave a big feast to his caste fellows. Bawan Ram managed the employment of his two sons-in-law in the same factory. Then he desired that his son should be an engineer. Therefore, he did not arrange the marriage of his son at an early age as per custom. However, after passing the intermediate standard, Anukul wanted to take admission to IIT, Delhi. It was a mere chance that, that year the students belonging to Scheduled Castes (SCs) were allowed to be admitted without appearing in the common admission test. Therefore, Bawan Ram took him to Delhi and went to the house of a local Member of Parliament (MP). There he found that the response of the MP was not as warm as he expected. However, the MP did recognise the significance of Bawan Ram, who had helped him in the last general elections by ensuring his castemen's votes. However, other visitors belonging to upper castes, who were also present there, insulted Bawan Ram and Anukul on the ground of untouchability. Further, MP's wife and his staff also insulted them by not allowing them to stay there and enjoy the common facilities during daytime. The MP belonged to a backward caste and hence he also realised the pains of caste prejudice. He once told Bawan Ram: "The only difference between the dalits and backwards is that our ancestors were given food in separate utensils whereas it was thrown before you people".[33] He further added, "They (upper caste people) sexually exploit others' women ... if not successful, they kill them. If legal action is initiated, they would blame the victim girl for her desire to tease and get raped. Bloody, liars? I say that the fire is about to burn".[34] The MP made a *pairvi* (recommendation) to a government official concerned, who told Bawan Ram frankly that the medium of instruction in IIT was English and, further, most of the students could not cope with the higher standard of education and, therefore, they committed suicide and also that despite a meagre scholarship, the overall expenditure would be very high.

Second, after taking admission, Anukul stayed in a hostel and his room partner was a boy belonging to scavenger community. When Anukul wrote about this to his parents, his mother became very disturbed because the place of the scavengers is at the bottom of the social hierarchy and the Chamar caste people would boycott Bawan Ram's family. Anukul also wrote that he and other students, belonging to SCs, were usually ridiculed by the upper caste students for coming from the reserved quota. Some students of other countries were also admitted under reserved quota without appearing in common admission test but they were not ridiculed because they spoke in English. Some of them were black Africans. Anukul further wrote about ragging by senior students and in the name of ragging they tortured the freshers. However, one old student, Ram Ujagir, belonging to SC, helped the freshers. Students from other castes feared him due to his vast and deep knowledge. Anukul also wrote that there every course was taught in English medium and, therefore, he had some difficulty to grasp that in the beginning but he hoped that he would overcome it.

Third, Anukul and other SC students felt an inferiority complex due to their inability to speak in English and to understand the subject matter taught in English medium. Therefore, Ram Ujagir suggested to the SC students that to compete with upper castes' students, the SC people should send their children to Convent schools from the very beginning because Indians were very liberal in making a foreign language or a foreign woman as their mother. He also suggested that temporarily they should have such names of their children as Mary and Christ so that the dictatorship of Hinduism could be controlled. Further, he also told them that there was no use of being a devotee and singing the songs of Kabir. He even criticised Gandhi, who tried to assuage the feelings of upper castes due to the anger of the SCs and gave the latter a new name 'Harijan'. He also criticised Bhim Rao Ambedkar, who ultimately agreed to Gandhiji's views.[35] This sermon had some effect on Anukul, who declared, "I think self-respect is greater than a man".[36] But he wanted to move slowly for bringing social change so that others' feelings are not hurt otherwise the conflict would be intensified.

Fourth, one day when Anukul was moving towards another corner of the hostel of the Institute along with his room partner, other students (belonging to upper castes) called them to identify a bad smell considering them to be experts in recognising smell. One of the students shook hands with Anukul, and later looked at both sides of his hands and then put them in his pocket. At this other students laughed but Arukul reacted sharply: "Go and wash your hands ..."[37] Another student tried to tease Anukul and his room partner Babu Ram by again requesting to recognise a bad smell. Babu Ram wanted to reply something in English but he could not utter it. Another student then remarked sarcastically "Everybody's intelligence is limited. Perhaps your intelligence may work when our intelligence does not work."[38]

Fifth, it was a student, named Mohan hanging from the ceiling fan.[39] He was also a student from the SC cluster. On his death, Ram Ujagir reacted: "Those students die who are either compelled to die or those who can convert their death into martyrdom."[40] When the authorities of the Institute turned up, one student remarked that they did not do anything worthwhile in time to prevent such events but when one student died they had turned up promptly. One student reacted at the Registrar, who was a Hindi writer: "Bloody Hindi writer wanted to bring Hindi in the national Institute to destroy it. Is it a language? In this language, one could be abused and vegetables could be purchased only. We should wage a war against this Hindi protagonist. The entire faculty is against him. He knows only obstruction in the name of administration."[41] When the police came, they did not show any concern to take down the dead body from the ceiling fan. Police wanted to get some clue about Mohan's love affair as the probable cause of suicide. Further, the police officer remarked that that was the third suicide case in three years; if the students did not want to study, why should they continue in that prestigious institute? Interestingly, the *'daroga'* (Sub-Inspector of Police) sarcastically remarked, "If there is no clue, get it written by the dead body which will obey the dictates of police."[42] Finally, Ram Ujagir took lead to take the dead body down. Other students did not dare to help him. When a police constable named Kallu wanted two extra persons for help, the Sub-inspector abused him, "Oh, a son of Dom! you were carrying the dead bodies life-long; now when you are recruited in the Police, so you bastard require two more persons."[43] Ram Ujagir also requested the

Sub-Inspector to help. At this the Sub-Inspector took the initiative but reacted that in his service even the upper caste is not respected. At this, Ram Ujagir reacted that he should resign and do the tasks of a priest, then nobody would request him to take down the corpse.

Sixth, after a few days things started moving in a routine manner but Ram Ujagir became ill. One day one student named Khanna teased Anukul by reminding him of his traditional occupation and warning him not to be a leader of SCs and Scheduled Tribes (STs). Khanna was the son of a senior officer, therefore the authorities of the Institute could not take action against him. When Ram Ujagir became seriously ill, his father took him back to his native place for treatment.

Seventh, one day Khanna caught hold of the collar of Anukul and asked: "Do you want to revolt against the system."[44] At this, Anukul told him that he had just organised a meeting of students of SCs and STs to discuss about their problems like non-payment of stipend. However, when Khanna abused him, Anukul asked him to mind his language. At this Khanna warned him of dire consequences. Next day, Anukul was beaten up by Khanna and his bone got fractured, hence he was hospitalised.

Eighth, Anukul's father Bawan Ram went to see him and started criticising Anukul because he had sent him to the national institute for personal upliftment by getting good education and not indulging in politics. When Bawan Ram was to be accommodated in the guest house, he had some reservation because of his belonging to low caste but Neelamma, an upper caste colleague of his Ram Ujagir, assured him that there would be no problem. However, she faced a lot of problems in getting a room in the guest house because the concerned official argued that Anukul wanted to kill Khanna and in that attempt he got himself fractured. Further, he also argued, Anukul's father had brought *goondas* along with him to beat Khanna. Even the Dean of Students Welfare had also some apprehension as he could not annoy upper caste students. But after a lot of persuasion by Neelamma, one room was allotted to Bawan Ram. However, he was again harassed there by Khanna and his friends who poisoned his ears about Neelamma's morality. Bawan Ram requested Neelamma that she belonged to an upper caste and, therefore, she should not make Anukul a pawn in the game. At this Neelamma told him frankly and boldly that he should not have any wrong opinion about her character. She also told him that she was not interested in Anukul in any form. Therefore, he could take him wherever he liked. She just wanted to help him because of being a human being. She also later remarked to Anukul bluntly: "Excuse me, the males have the same attitude towards women as the upper castes have about the untouchables."[45]

Ninth, one day, Neelamma decided to visit the village of Ram Ujagir because his condition had deteriorated badly. When she reached Ram Ujagir's house, most of the people again suspected her character. Even his mother and brother-in-law's wife too suspected her. There people believed that one spirit or magic was harassing Ram Ujagir, hence some witchcraft's help should be taken for his treatment. Further, one child told her that Ram Ujagir had studied a lot, therefore he was being victimised by the Satan. Furthermore, some thought that due to upper castes' curse he was suffering. Then she found pigs roaming around and many children were moving about naked. There was no chair in the house, therefore she was offered a cot. But Neelamma told Ram Ujagir not to have an inferiority complex because of lack of facilities. Neelamma found that the mother of Ram Ujagir was worried for him. Further, she consoled her that she should not worry as Ram Ujagir was a brave man. But his mother's low caste syndrome was reflected in her statement: "A curse of higher caste has made Ram Ujagir so."[46] There, Neelamma also came to know that when Ram Ujagir had fits of madness, he attempted to commit suicide. Later, Ram Ujagir's sister told Neelamma that she did not go to school – because it was looked down by the community and the school-going girls were considered characterless. But Neelamma told her that if one went to school, one's fear went away. Ram Ujagir had developed a phobia of upper caste people because of the earlier incident of suicide by Mohan. He cursed upper caste people as "the enemies of the possibilities".[47] Neelamma also found that in the village Ram Ujagir was treated by witchcraft, not by modern doctors. She also realised that Ram Ujagir had become very emotional and with too much affection from family members and no initiative of his own had taken him into the tunnel of darkness. Then, suggesting for modern treatment at the Institute, she went back to the Institute when his family members refused to take him there. Later, she wrote letters, to Ram Ujagir that he would have to "revolt against himself" in order to come out of the darkness.

Tenth, so Ram Ujagir went to join the Institute. But Neelamma had left for joining the post of a lecturer in South India. Ram Ujagir did not get support in academics nor any arrangement could be done about his mess facility. He wrote a letter to Neelamma that he was like a matchstick which was burning bright before becoming ashes and he also wrote that he was a born Hindu and could not change it. He also wrote a letter to his father that if one found that struggle was heavier than himself, he should not go back rather should become a martyr. He wrote the third letter to Anukul that he did not get courage and self-respect in heritage. He also appreciated Anukul because he had restlessness to change the situation instead of just cursing and hating it. He also wrote that he should convince his (Ram Ujagir's) parents that he wanted to get rid of the debt of mother and father but had very little time. Thereafter, he committed suicide by hanging himself from the ceiling fan. At the death of Ram Ujagir, the authorities of the Institute kept silence and the daily newspapers published that news. They simply said that on the application of Ram Ujagir, a final decision was yet to be taken and his suicide had personal reasons.

Eleventh, when Neelamma got a telegram from Anukul about Ram Ujagir's suicide, she became angry at his cowardly deed but ultimately she went there where most of the students were of the view that it was not a suicide by Ram Ujagir but a 'killing by the society'. A committee was formed by the Institute to trace out the reasons of the suicide by Ram Ujagir. Anukul declared in the condolence meeting that if situation remained so, each and every lamp would extinguish. However, he declared that if the students wanted to do something, they should do self-introspection. The committee formed by the institute reported that because of his bad performance in examinations and personal problems as well as failure of a love affair with an upper caste girl, Ram Ujagir had committed suicide; the teachers in the Institute were well qualified, and the administrators had no discrimination against anybody. The report concluded that due to suicide by Ram Ujagir, the image and reputation of the institute was damaged.

Twelfth, when father of Ram Ujagir received copy of the report sent by the Institute (in English), he replied to the enquiry officer that he was considered low by the entire society but he was "not low in his own eyes". Further he also wrote that the students and teachers of upper castes/classes compelled his son to commit suicide. He also wrote that he should not be called to the institute further. Finally, he wrote that Anukul was like a god for his son Ram Ujagir, therefore, the institute's authorities should save him and ensure that he went back safely to his parents. Thus, he requested the authorities not to give any letter to him again, otherwise his wounds would get further aggravated. Here the novel ends.

Inner Connections

The novelist tries to forge a unity of dalits and backward class to fight the oppression at the hands of the upper castes. One may read between the lines when the local MP Mr Chaudhuri tells Bawan Ram at his Delhi residence that both dalits and the backwards suffer from the wound inflicted by the upper castes and in this regard the difference between the two is only a matter of degree – dalits' wound is deeper than that of the backward class. Secondly, some of the backwards like wife of the MP also discriminate against the dalits in their day-to-day life. Thirdly, there exists intra-dalit discrimination also; for example, Anukul's mother strongly reacts to her son's staying with a scavenger boy because of her relatively higher status in the caste hierarchy and also a fear of ex-communication from her community. Modern educational institutions follow the western language (English) in letter and spirit but they also, practise traditional caste prejudices against dalits like Ram Ujagir and Anukul, thus dalits suffer doubly.

A sociological analysis of these novels will be attempted in next chapter.

Notes and References

1. Munshi Premchand (1999), *Rangbhumi*, Hans Prakashan, Allahabad, p. 9.
2. Ibid., p. 112.
3. Ibid., p. 116.
4. Ibid., p. 118.
5. Ibid., p. 315.
6. Ibid., p. 331.
7. Ibid., p. 190.
8. Ibid.
9. Ibid., p. 428.
10. Ibid., p. 468.
11. Ibid., p. 488.
12. Pandey Bechan Sharma 'Ugra' (1925), *Budhua Ki Beti*, Bisawin Sadi Pustakalaya, Calcutta (Kolkata).
13. Ibid., p. 1.
14. Ibid., p. 5.
15. Ibid., p. 128.
16. Ibid., pp. 139–40.
17. Ibid., pp. 213–15.
18. Ibid., p. 295.
19. Ibid., p. 337.
20. Ibid., p. 338.
21. Ibid., pp. 338–39.
22. Ibid., pp. 344–45.

23. Jagdish Chandra (1996), *Dharti Dhan Na Apna*, Raj Kamal Prakashan Pvt. Ltd. (Paperback), New Delhi, p. 4.
24. Ibid., p. 7.
25. Ibid., p. 8.
26. Ibid., p. 9.
27. Ibid., p. 27.
28. Ibid., p. 29.
29. Ibid., p. 94.
30. Ibid., pp. 191–92.
31. Giriraj Kishor (1984), *Parishishta*, Raj Kamal Prakashan, New Delhi, p. 4.
32. Ibid., p. 9.
33. Ibid., p. 61.
34. Ibid.
35. Ibid., p. 113.
36. Ibid., p. 114.
37. Ibid., p. 115.
38. Ibid., p. 116.
39. Ibid.
40. Ibid., p. 117.
41. Ibid., p. 119.
42. Ibid., p. 120.
43. Ibid., p. 123.
44. Ibid., p. 154.
45. Ibid., p. 195.
46. Ibid., p. 209.
47. Ibid., p. 212.

6

A Sociological Analysis of Selected Novels

We have already described the textual structures of four selected novels in the previous chapter. Now, we will try to present their sociological contexts. This sociological analysis may be attempted in the following terms:

(a) Socio-cultural base of dalit characters.

(b) Dalit and non-dalit interaction.

(c) Do Dalits protest or not?

(d) Novelist's background and vision(s).

(e) Which sort of realism works? – analysis of the message conveyed by each novel.

Now, we will analyse the selected four novels in the light of these issues:

Rangbhumi

Socio-cultural Base

The socio-cultural base of the novel, *Rangbhumi* is rural. Its theme is the beginning of the process of industrialisation – establishment of a factory in a village, namely, Pandepur (Banaras) by acquiring the housesites as well as the entire land of the village. Different castes such as *Brahman* (Naik Ram Panda) and *Rajput* (K. Bharat Singh, Mahendra Kumar, etc.) as Upper

Castes, *Ahir* (Bajrangi), *Bania* (Jagdhar) and *Tamoli* (Thakurdin) as backward castes, *Chamar* (Surdas, Mithua) and *Pasi* (Bhairo, Subhagi) as lower castes (dalits) are depicted in this novel. In terms of religion, three major religions of India, Hinduism, Islam and Christianity are well represented here. In terms of racial background, English officials (Mr Clark) and Indians are depicted in this novel. As far as gender is concerned, both male and female characters are depicted. The range of the novel expands from a village, namely Pandepur, to the city of Banaras (Varanasi) and then to Rajputana (Rajasthan), Punjab, Garhwal and Poona.

Interaction

There are both intra-dalit and dalit with non-dalit interactions in this novel. On the one hand, within the Dalit community there is both cooperation and conflict; for example, Surdas (belonging to a Chamar caste) is harassed by another dalit, Bhairo, belonging to Pasi caste, by committing theft in the hut of former and, by accusing him of having illicit relationship with his wife, Subhagi and eventually getting him punished by the Honorary Magistrate. On the contrary, despite such attempts on his character assassination, Surdas gives shelter to Subhagi as his sister. There is inter-caste conflict in terms of attempting to outrage the modesty of Subhagi by two youths belonging to backward community (Vidyadhar and Ghisu). On this issue, Surdas does not compromise despite the pressure from the society and gets them punished, so that nobody in future would dare to outrage the modesty of women. Further, unlike the traditional village social structure in India, in Pandepur there are no separate settlements for different castes, especially for dalits. Moreover, all the villagers of different castes take part in social and religious functions, like reciting of devotional songs (bhajans) wherein the role of blind Surdas is very significant. Another dalit, Bhairo, also participates in that collective function. He is appreciated by all the village persons including Naik Ram Panda, belonging to the highest Brahmin caste. Surdas also takes milk, etc., from different villagers (especially from Bajrangi) free of cost for his nephew, Mithua. Here caste divisions exist but without conflict. Thus, Surdas, even though he belongs to dalit community, does not face caste prejudices. Therefore, socially he is in the core group of the society, not on the margin. In reality, on the basis of 'achievement' qualities like sacrifice, truthfulness, helpfulness, etc., (instead of ascription), Surdas gets more respect from all. Even John Sewak, against whom Surdas had fought a long-drawn struggle due to the acquisition of his land by force, goes to the hospital (where Surdas is admitted) and begs his pardon for his inhuman conduct. Not only this, Sophia, daughter of John Sewak, appreciated Surdas from the very beginning because of his many moral qualities. Even the tough and dictator-like District Collector, Mr Clark is also afraid of persons like Surdas and repents that he had taken coercive action against such persons as those whose European counterparts commanded his respect. At the death of Surdas, Mr Clark says to Mahendra Kumar: "I fear not persons like you, but such persons (as Surdas) who rule on the people's heart. It is a repentance of ruling here that in this country (India) we kill those persons whom we would have thought as god-like" (p. 523). Thus, non-dalits respect him more than even dalits do.

Protest

Dalits have protested against their exploitation. The central dalit character, Surdas, has protested time and again when his land as well as housesite were acquired by a capitalist, namely, John Sevak, through the district administration. There in the protest itself, he is killed by the bullet of the Collector. Surdas protested the land acquisition by force and without due payment on following grounds:

(a) It is his ancestral property to be preserved, not to be disposed of;

(b) It is an open land used as pasture for the village animals;

(c) It cannot be disposed of without the consent of the villagers; and

(d) He also wanted to construct a drinking well there for the use of passers-by and villagers.

Secondly, Subhagi, another dalit character, and Surdas caught hold of two village youths (Vidyadhar and Ghisu) when the latter tried to outrage her modesty at night in the house of Surdas, where she had taken shelter. Further, despite request by the villagers to excuse the two accused boys, Surdas refused straight-forwardly and got them punished under the rule of law.

Thirdly, Bhairo accuses Surdas for having illicit relationship with his wife Subhagi and complains to the Honorary Magistrate, Raja Mahendra Kumar, who without making an impartial enquiry punishes both Surdas and Subhagi by fining them. But Surdas protests against this injustice before the court itself. Then a large number of people gather over there and they support Surdas economically and morally. They collect subscription voluntarily and make payment of the fine imposed.

However, in these three events though the victims are from the dalit community yet the fact remains that they are victimised not simply because they are dalits. In the first event, Surdas' land is forcibly acquired along with other villagers' lands for industrialisation – especially for construction of a cigarette factory. Second event takes place when the two youths, from backward community, find it easy to exploit Subhagi where she was alone because Surdas, being a blind man, was not perceived to be a real obstruction. In the third event, Bhairo himself is a dalit and accuses another dalit for allegedly exploiting his wife.

Novelist's Background and Vision

Premchand was born in a lower-middle class family of Kayastha caste (an upper caste in Hindu caste system) in a village called Lemahi in Banaras in 1880. He was educated up to graduate level (BA) and was working as a teacher and Deputy Inspector of Schools under the British Government. This novel was written by him during 1922–1924. This was the period when Indian National Congress got the leadership of Mahatma Gandhi, who turned the one-dimensional movement, limited to urban areas and the educated class only, to the masses in the vast rural areas. He also introduced new techniques of protest – non-violence, civil disobedience, demonstration, boycott of foreign goods, government jobs and government organisations like schools. He visited different parts of the country for actively involving the people at large. One such visit was at Gorakhpur (UP) on the 8 February 1921, where Gandhiji delivered a passionate patriotic speech which impressed the writer Premchand very much. Therefore, on the 15 February 1921, he resigned from the government job after serving for about 21 years under the British rule. Before this, his one collection of stories, namely, *'Soj-e-watan'*, published in Urdu, was seized by the British Collector alleging it to be anti-government in spirit. Since then Premchand started writing in Hindi and changed his name from Nawab Rai to Premchand to avoid government's wrath.

As far as his vision is concerned, he had a clear vision about the liberation of India from the British rule in general and that of masses from *zamindars* and capitalists in particular. In this novel, *Rangbhumi* the central character, Surdas, seems to be inspired and influenced by Mahatma Gandhi who stood for the common people of the villages and against the British government. Surdas is one of the most common characters who is economically poor, peasant by occupation, belonging to the lower caste of Chamar (dalit), physically handicapped (blind), illiterate and a beggar. However, despite being weak he has extraordinary qualities such as having consideration for others, strong will power, moral values, capability to struggle time and again, etc. He applies non-violence as a legitimate means for legitimate ends, does not tell a lie and has a lot of self-confidence.

On analysis of the novel, following points regarding his vision emerge:

(a) Premchand is not bound by the middle class syndrome. Therefore, he transcends his social, cultural and economic background and makes a man from lower caste and class as the central character of the novel.

(b) His vision goes beyond the limited area of towns to the vast areas of villages wherein the soul of India lives (Gandhiji).

(c) He takes the side of women like Subhagi who are exploited by their husbands and the rules of patriarchy. Thus, he is for women's rights.

(d) Through Surdas, Premchand has depicted the then national freedom struggle against the British rule. Like Indian National Congress there are both liberals and radicals in this novel who oppose the British policy of industrialisation at the cost of eviction of the villagers.

(e) Premchand has shown the nexus between the capitalist class (John Sevak), zamindar class (Kunwar Bharat Singh, Mahendra Kumar) and the colonial power (Mr Clark). Premchand has also been successful in presenting instances of transcendence of class; for example, Sophia moves herself away from the capitalist class and Vinay from the zamindar class – a process of 'declassing'. Further, Sophia, a Christian, shows her likeness for freedom to choose one of many gods in Hinduism.

Type of Realism and Message

Here, the realism depicted by Premchand is neither strictly 'socialist realism' nor 'critical realism'. He was impressed by Gandhiji and Arya Samaj in his real life and in this novel Premchand appears with his voice of a true nationalist and a true writer of India's national freedom struggle. He has not depicted realism in a status quoist and naked form, i.e., naturalism because he found different shades of reality existing side by side as well as the potentialities to change and, therefore, he brought authenticity by depicting different dimensions of different characters in *Rangbhumi*. He has not made Surdas a hero deliberately by showing some of his weaknesses also though his strength is more highlighted than his weakness. For instance, Surdas owns 10 bighas of land and can get sufficient food for his living by giving this land on share-cropping to someone in the village but he is not shown doing so, rather he earns his living by begging. Secondly, though his nephew Mithua is in a bad company, he has burnt Bhairo's shop and also does not care for Surdas, yet while admitted in the hospital and lying on his death bed, he asked Mithua whether he would perform all the rituals for him or not because he was the only heir from his family and caste. Thus, he is still conscious of his family, religions and caste rites. Thirdly, Surdas is very much anxious to go to Gaya for *'tarpan'* (salvation) of his ancestors. This concern for the dead, that is past, that is history, is an element of Indian tradition which has been quite realistically presented by Prem Chand.

Premchand's realism lies in between idealistic realism and critical realism. Premchand's *Rangbhumi* has peasants, untouchables and women as groups. Therefore, group character is significant but at the same time the character of Surdas is prominently depicted with various positive qualities of a hero (though he may not be called a hero, he is certainly a central character). Surdas rallies groups and individuals against the colonial design. Therefore, Premchand's realism may be called 'humanistic critical realism'.

One finds following messages from *Rangbhumi:*

(a) Industrialisation is not the panacea for all problems like poverty, unemployment, etc., because the promoters of industrialisation intend to open only those factories which are more and more profit-oriented irrespective of the fact whether they give due employment or not.

(b) One finds a struggle for protecting the women's dignity from the clutches of bad persons. It is not women's liberation of western type where women are often in total opposition to the males. Rather, here Premchand depicts women's emancipation through male (Surdas)-female (Subhagi) partnership with a genuine cause. This incisive insight is very appreciable, especially during the first quarter of 20th century.

(c) National freedom struggle (depicted in the activities of Sewa Samiti) is the most important for all the castes and communities and though the novel's main locus is centred in Banaras (Varanasi), the struggle expands to Rajputana (Rajasthan), Punjab, Garhwal and Poona (Pune).

(d) One finds a broad representation of Indian social reality in this novel in terms of a large number of characters from different backgrounds – social, economic, educational, political, religious, etc.
(e) Though hero is not very essential in a novel, yet the central character matters in terms of his or her qualities of achievements and especially his or her vision of the society.
(f) The novel depicts social life in a complicated and complex way, therefore realism of this novel is also complicated, complex and multidimensional. In short, a novel cannot be a shortcut genre of realism as human life is never shortcut. In terms of both range and depth, therefore, *Rangbhumi* is a big novel. However, to be more specific, its range also covers to some insignificant events such as Tahir Ali's family affairs, closeness of Sophia and Clark leading to their visit to Udaipur without being married, etc. Similarly, in order to show his patriotism, events such as suicide of Vinay Singh, coincidence of the meeting of Vinay and Sophia in the railway compartment while returning from Udaipur, Vinay and Sophia staying in a tribal village in Rajputana maintaining chastity despite the use of some indigenous medicines for hypnotising Sophia by Vinay seem to be unrealistic.
(g) Premchand seems to stand for the liberation of all deprived sections like peasants, women, untouchables (dalits), illiterates in their fight against the nexus of the capitalists, *zamindars* and imperialists.
(h) Finally, Premchand stands for progressive and scientific vision by opposing superstitions, communal prejudices, caste biases and other parochial and primordial ties.

Budhua ki Beti

Socio-cultural Base

The novel *Budhua ki Beti* is based on the urban society of Banaras (now Varanasi) in UP. Different castes like Brahman

(Aghori), Rajput (Ghanshyam), Kayastha as well as dalits (Bhangis like Budhua) figure in this novel. As far as religions are concerned, three major religions of India – Hinduism, Islam and Christianity – are very well depicted there. Even in terms of race, English officials like Mr Young (District Judge) and his wife, Mrs Young, as well as other European characters are depicted. Similarly, both male and female characters, literate and illiterate, young and old ones are depicted. Though the novel begins and centres around Banaras city, it ends with the departure of one main female character, Radha, to Europe along with Mr Young as his heiress.

Interaction

There are both intra-dalit and dalit with non-dalit interactions in the novel. Radha, being a dalit girl, is sexually exploited by an upper caste man, Ghanshyam (Rajput) while Aghori Manushyanand, belonging to another higher caste (Brahman), is whole-heartedly helping the untouchables' liberation as a catalyst. He openly defies old traditional customs and sanctions against the untouchables. The messiah of the dalits, B.R. Ambedkar, became active on the national scene for launching a movement of dalits' temple entry in 1930 for the first time in Indian history. But before that in 1928 itself, novelist 'Ugra' allowed dalits' entry to Vishwanath temple in Banaras in his novel, *Budhua ki Beti* under the inspiration of a central character, Aghori Manushyanand. That shows that as an author, 'Ugra' was much ahead of his time. Further, about fifty volunteers inspired by Aghori Baba worked tirelessly for the emancipation of dalits, though they hailed from upper castes and middle class background. Furthermore, there is close interaction between Hindus and Christians as shown by the characters such as Aghori Baba and the priest of the church, Father Johnson, Aghori Baba and Mr Young (District Judge). Further, Liakat Hussain and Rahman from the Muslim community have negative interaction and they sexually exploit Budhua's wife, Sukli, on the pretext of blessing her with a son through the angels. But interestingly, Budhua's daughter helps and cares when Liakat

Hussain suffers from illness and starvation later. She and Aghori Baba give him shelter in the Ashram. Further, within dalits themselves, there are different opinions – old generation of dalits, more often, want a peaceful compromise while the young generation is in a mood to revolt against the system itself. While the old generation of non-dalits believes in status quo, their young generation is ready to give a better space for dalits in the prevailing relationship.

Protest

In this novel, sweepers were organised by the inspiration of Aghori Baba and under the leadership of Budhua from amongst themselves to fight against the social, economic and cultural oppression of the upper castes. First, they make a symbolic protest and later they go on strike and do not clean individual and public latrines, drains, roads, etc. The administration – both civil and police – fails in negotiations with them. They later return to work only when their demands of building new houses, enhancement of wages, construction of a new temple, opening of a new school, imparting new technical skills to their youth are accepted with dignity. Thus, their demands are multidimensional; social, economic and cultural. But it is interesting to note that in the beginning when a Vaidya (a person practising Ayurveda) and allopathic doctors refused to treat Budhua's first wife on the ground of untouchability (social cause) and also because of his poverty (economic cause), Budhua decided to make an individual protest by declaring not to clean the latrines of any Vaidya or doctor even if he has to clean the excreta of dogs. This individual protest later gets more organised and collective mobilisation takes the form of social protest that is inspired and organised by Aghori Baba but led by Budhua with collective participation of the dalit masses. The success of their collective strike, a direct conflict, clearly shows the way for future action.

Novelist's Background and Vision

Ugra was born on 29 December 1900, in Mirzapur (UP) and died in 1967. He was born in a Brahman family with lower middle class background in rural area. While studying he had composed a poem on Mahatma Gandhi. Further, he wrote a story, *Gandhi Ashram*. That shows influence of Gandhism on him. He also joined the national freedom struggle and went to jail. However, he became disillusioned with Gandhian liberalism (1923–1924) and talked of even violent means for nation's liberation. His stories, *Swadesh Ke Liye* (1923), *Wah Din* and *Sundari Hinsa* (1924) were in this spirit, and these were a critique of Gandhian philosophy of non-violence. He used to write revolutionary stories as he was very much impressed by the Soviet Revolution of 1917. However, he did not join any socialist political organisation. He joined 'Matwala' group of non-conformist writers in Kolkata. His first anthology of revolutionary stories, namely, *Chingariyan* was published in 1926. Out of twelve stories of this collection, six were concerned with the background of Soviet Revolution while the remaining six were based on Indian freedom struggle. But because of its revolutionary appeal, it was seized by the British government on 26 May 1928.[1] Ugra remained unmarried and, therefore, believed in unrestricted sexuality, even to the extent of prostitution. In childhood, he used to take part in Ramlila (a dramatic folk re-enactment of the life story of Lord Rama) both as Lakshman and Sita.

Ugra was moderately educated and he gave due space to poverty, sexual exploitation and untouchability in his writings. When he edited *Vijaya* issue of *Swadesh* in October, 1924, it was seized and a case was instituted against him and others for waging a war against the State and then he was punished for 9 months' imprisonment. Ugra had joined active journalism and his ideal was V.V. Paradkar, the editor of *Aaj*. He did not believe in the theory of 'art for art sake' rather his literature had a revolutionary ethos against British rulers, exploiters of women and the caste system.[2] His multidimensional vision is reflected in *Budhua ki Beti* which is both a creative work of dalits' discourse and women's discourse. Though Premchand had written *Rangbhumi* earlier in 1925, depicting a dalit blind man, namely Surdas, as central character, yet dalits' discourse per se was not the theme of that novel. On the other hand, *Budhua ki Beti* is purely a dalit discourse, by a non-dalit writer who, despite having no direct self-experience, has been successful in depicting dalits' and women's exploitation simultaneously by having 'empathy', in word and deed. His one of the main characters, Aghori Baba transcends his middle class and upper caste (Brahman) background while inspiring the exploited dalit masses as a catalyst. Ugra sincerely realised that caste system was very complex, therefore to break it he created the character of Aghori Baba who, being *Aghori,* did not believe in untouchability. Thus Ugra, through Aghori Baba, has been successful to liberate the lowest caste of sweepers in the hierarchised Hindu social order.

Type of Realism and Message

Ugra has been accused of naturalism and naked depiction by many critics in Hindi literature like Benarsidas Chaturvedi,[3] Nalin V. Sharma,[4] etc. However, it is not true at least in the novel of *Budhua ki Beti* because he has just not photographed the social reality as it exists in naked form, rather he also shows the potentialities and possibilities of the downtrodden untouchables and women. In fact, he was an activist writer who participated in the movement of freedom struggle as well as literary movement for social change. His novel is explosive and ahead of his time and therefore, many of his colleagues and contemporary critics could not digest his revolting writings like *Budhua ki Beti*. During 1920s, national movement of freedom struggle had two streams of action – liberal and radical. Ugra highlighted the radical side of social reality in order to bring structural social changes in the system. He had a creative energy to diagnose the existing social problems vividly and minutely. Therefore, he has gone into the depth of social situation of untouchability. His novel's range is not very large, but its depth is certainly very much. Therefore, his novel, *Budhua ki Beti* and other writings had a large section of readers and his writings had many editions. He transcended his high caste background and captured the delicate and minute shades of reality by empathising with the untouchables and women. Although he had no direct experience yet he had a forward-looking vision. The type of realism depicted there is 'subaltern realism', as Gopal Roy says (Chapter 1). The messages of the novel are as follows:

(a) The upper castes have to give due space to the downtrodden dalits in a dignified way.
(b) Dalits' liberation demands multidimensional strategy (social, economic, political and cultural) simultaneously so that the exploiters may not take undue advantage of their subordinate position in a society in one way or other.
(c) Women are as much downtrodden as untouchables; therefore, they deserve a similar kind of liberation.
(d) Christianity does not believe in untouchability as Hinduism and Islam do in practice in India. Though, according to the novelist, Christian missionaries may be appreciated for having positive view towards untouchables as far as appropriate interaction is concerned, yet they have also a narrow motive of conversion of the downtrodden untouchables. Therefore, in the ultimate analysis they are also not true and genuine friends of dalits.
(e) Dalits are so much oppressed that the leadership for social change does not emerge on its own, rather it requires a catalyst agent from outside in order to inspire and mobilise them in such a way that after sometime when the movement gets momentum a genuine leadership may emerge from amongst themselves.

Parishishta

Socio-cultural Base

The novel, *Parishishta* was published in 1984. It is based on a village in western UP but extends to an urban area in western UP where Bawan Ram is working in a factory. Later, it extends to Delhi where there is an IIT wherein central character, Anukul Ram, takes admission to Engineering course of study. In this novel, there are several dalits – Anukul

Ram, his father Bawan Ram, Parvati (mother of Anukul), Ram Ujagir, his father Suvaran Choudhary – and upper castes like Rajendra Singh (MP), Khanna, Nilamma, Prof. Malkani as well as backwards like Mr Choudhary (Member of Parliament). Bawan Ram is educated only up to eighth standard but Parvati is illiterate.

Interaction

The novelist has depicted intra-dalit and dalit with non-dalit interaction very vividly. Dalit characters such as Ram Ujagir and Anukul fight for the cause of dalits wholeheartedly but another dalit, a Balmiki boy (Baburam) is unable to fight the exploitation and ultimately escapes. Though Nilamma and Prof. Malkani belong to upper castes, they have true empathy for dalits. However, Bawan Ram, because of less education and rural socialisation, suspects Nilamma of influencing his son Anukul for making love. Similarly, Ram Ujagir's mother, sister-in-law and other family members as well as villagers also suspect her of influencing him for making love. But the truth is otherwise. Therefore, Nilamma clarifies her position strongly at both places. She represents women's category as far as exploitation is concerned but at the same time she transcends her caste background (Brahmin) and takes the side of dalits, Ram Ujagir and Anukul. She fights for the accommodation for Anukul's father with the establishment. Thus, she identifies her cause of women with that of dalits for a united struggle against the exploitation of caste and patriarchy. Similarly, Prof. Malkani, a non-dalit, supports Ram Ujagir. On the other hand, upper caste students like Khanna and authorities discriminate against dalits.

Protest

In this novel dalit students protest when they are taunted by the upper caste students who remind them of their forefathers' traditional dirty occupations of leather works, etc. Further, they also protest when they are abused and assaulted by Khanna and his team. When the administration of the Institute tries to ignore the death of Ram Ujagir (a dalit student), the dalit students and their parents with the support of some non-dalit students like Nilamma and non-dalit teachers like Prof. Malkani protest against them and declare it as a death forced by the society against its system. Ram Ujagir protests with a zeal against the exploitative system in his daily life but ultimately he surrenders due to the pressure of adverse circumstances imposed by the Institute in terms of not allowing his readmission. Difference between the protest by Anukul and Ram Ujagir is expressed in the letter that Ram Ujagir wrote before his death: "I was struggling with enthusiasm while you are struggling with an understanding .... You have restlessness to change, not hatred against your circumstances. You have within yourselves a long-drawn struggle, not a revolt of a spark. By change you mean to change from within while I thought only the outer change a change".[5] Thus it is clear that Ram Ujagir was the first dalit to sacrifice for the cause of the entire community and that cause is still pursued by Anukul in a more sustained struggle.

Novelist's Background and Vision

The novelist Giriraj Kishor was born in an Agrawal (trader) family in Muzaffarnagar (UP). He took higher education and got a job at IIT, Kanpur (as Director, Creative Writing and Publication Centre). He hailed from a middle caste and class. He believes: "There is nothing like Scheduled Caste, rather there is a scheduled mentality, whosoever is pushed aside by the elite class (which has hegemony), becomes the scheduled one." He transcends his middle caste and class background and empathises with the dalits. According to him, it is not necessary that for writing on dalits' consciousness, one has necessarily to be a dalit by birth, rather it is enough if one puts oneself in that situation and realises the pangs of the system minutely. The novelist has a futuristic vision to highlight the exploitation of the students from the downtrodden class, especially from rural areas. They have not only monetary problems in purchasing costly books and instruments but also social problems of interaction with higher caste and class students. They cannot speak sophisticated foreign language, namely, English, which is the medium of instruction in the technical institutions in India. Thus, the novelist does not merely depict the social reality from caste angle but also from class and cultural angles. Further, the author has been a keen observer while depicting the subordinate status of women in the society in general and educational institutions in particular. Actually, women face similar kind of obstacles as dalits do because both issues (caste and sex) are decided by birth.

Type of Realism and Message

The novelist has succeeded in realistically depicting various shades of realism at individual, group and society levels. For instance, Bawan Ram and his Chamar community has faced discrimination from non-dalits who considered them low. However, dalits also have intra-dalit hierarchy of discrimination and the Chamar community looks down upon Balmiki (sweeper) community. After taking admission in the IIT, Anukul finds there, one Balmiki student (Baburam) with whom nobody is ready to share a room in the hostel; therefore, Anukul decides to share the room with him. But when he discloses all this fact to his parents in a letter, his mother reacts strongly because, in her view, her caste is higher in the caste hierarchy and her family will be declared outcast by the entire Chamar community and, therefore, she requests her husband to write to Anukul to change the room somehow. Secondly, when Bawan Ram goes to Delhi for taking admission of his son through the help of the local Member of Parliament (MP), Mr Chaudhary (from backward caste), both father and son face disrespect from the upper caste visitors there, on the one hand, and MP's wife on the other. While MP's wife tries to keep a distance from Bawan Ram and Anukul on the basis of caste, the MP, Mr Choudhary, does not maintain that distance, rather he openly admits that he won the previous election with the help of Bawan Ram and his community's votes. Moreover, the MP stands for the unity of backwards and dalits as, in his view, in the exploitation of dalits and backwards, there is only a difference of degree – that is, while backwards are given food in different utensils of upper caste, dalits are not given utensils. But both realise the pangs of wounds and disrespect, though the wound of and disrespect to dalits is deeper than that of backwards. Thus, in this novel, the class, caste and cultural (language) exploitation go hand in hand. Therefore, realism depicted here is multi-dimensional cultural realism, but it is an Indianised cultural realism, wherein caste exploitation exists in addition to class exploitation. We get following messages from this novel:

(a) As existing in the society neither all upper castes are bad nor are all dalits good, hence a class viewpoint needs to be taken.

(b) The hegemony of English language should be broken and Hindi should be given due place and recognition in all the streams of life, including the higher educational institutes.

(c) Class differentiation/division is more important than caste differentiation/division.

(d) Despite the provision of reservation for the Scheduled Castes in educational institutions, the upper castes' mentality of looking down upon them still exists in society at large, though upper castes do not mind any kind of reservation for foreign students who speak English.

(e) The bureaucratisation of the higher educational institutions has badly damaged the budding talents in different ways but unfortunately the power-that-be of such institutions does not make any kind of introspection about its malfunctioning, rather it more often blames the students and their parents who are the victims of the system, for not coping with the requirements of the higher educational system.

Dharti Dhan Na Apna

Socio-cultural Base

The socio-cultural base of this novel is a village in Punjab. This village is divided into several settlements, especially those of the upper castes/middle castes, on the one hand and the Harijans on the other. The settlement of Harijans is known as 'Chamadari'. This reflects socio-cultural background of the village. However, the central character of the novel, Kali, had worked in Kanpur town and returned to his village after working there for six years. When he was away in the city, he had nostalgia for his village life but when he returned, he was disillusioned with the hard reality of village life. There are upper castes, middle castes like Jats, Bania and Kumbhkar and lower castes like Chamar. There are Hindu characters in majority, and Christian and Sikh characters in minority.

Interaction

There are both intra-dalit and dalit with non-dalit interactions, the latter leading to conflicts. Significant conflict is between Jats and Chamars, wherein trader and moneylender Chhajju Shah takes the side of Jats and does not provide money and material to Chamars who are struggling against the Jats in terms of boycotting their work due to non-payment of due wages. However, there are also intra-dalit conflicts. Two Chamar families of Mangu, who is the semi-bonded labour of Chaudhary Harnam Singh, and of Nikku and Prito are one side, supporting the landowners (because they are also benefited from Chaudhary Harnam Singh's family through Mangu) and Kali and other Chamars are on the other side. Further, there is an interaction of the village Chamars under the leadership of Kali with communist leaders of the region (Dr Bishan Das and Tahal Singh) and also with priests of the local church and temple. While the Hindu priest does not allow Chamars to take water from his drinking well at the time of crisis (when the drinking wells of Chamardari get sunk due to floods), the Church priest allows them to use his hand pump in the beginning but due to filth created by them the church priest's wife subsequently refuses them to use that. The communist leaders do not help them in crisis despite their favourable preachings. Similarly, the church priest does not solemnise the marriage of Kali and Gyano when she is pregnant and there is fear of ex-communication by the community. This shows that though he preaches for conversion of dalits in normal time, he does not help in a crisis. In this novel, there is no major conflict between upper caste and lower caste, rather there is one between middle caste of Jats and lower caste of Chamars at social and economic levels.

Protests

In this novel, there are two types of protests:

1. Social protest because of disrespect shown by Jats to Chamars; and
2. Economic protest because of non-payment of due wages to dalit labourers for their work.

However, it is also a notable fact that economic protest is more prominent because it is directly concerned with the question of survival of the Chamars and if they do not get wages due to them, they would starve. On the other hand, Chaudhary Harnam Singh starts beating Santu and Jitu (dalits) simply on the basis of his suspicion that the latter had damaged his maize crops. He abuses Chamars on several occasions, hence Kali protests.

Novelist's Background and Vision

The novelist was born in a middle class and caste family in a village in Punjab and got higher education. He spent most of his adolescent days in Ralhan, a village of his maternal uncle, in Punjab. There he found a Harijan settlement 'Chamadari' on the outskirts of the village. The upper/middle castes had to obey certain social sanctions and traditions while going to Harijans' settlement. But the author broke those sanctions by eating with a Chamar family. He was a student of Economics, therefore he used to see economic causes behind those social sanctions. Chamars did not have any right over the land they cultivated, and not even on the house-sites they lived on. He admits that he did not himself experience the cruel realities of a Harijan's life, yet he was successful in seeing them closely. He has empathised with the relevant references of the Harijans' life objectively and has not imposed his opinion or ideology on the story, as he admits so in the Introduction part of the novel. His vision is very deep indeed as he was the first Hindi novelist to depict Harijans' life so vividly, struggling in multidimensional ways. He has not been a slave of any ideology, political party or caste lobby. However, it may be said that the author's vision is limited to protests only, not to a full-fledged movement.

Type of Realism and Message

The author has depicted various shades of social reality and the realism depicted here is close to the dialectics of Marxist realism wherein social, political and economic forces complement each other in a dialectical way. Here, class exploitation is supplemented by caste exploitation, hence it is an Indianised Marxist realism. But his realism is not of an orthodox Marxist type because he has not praised uncritically the communist leaders like, Tahal Singh and Dr Bishan Das, who do not help Kali and his fellows who are struggling against the feudal landlords socially and economically. While most of the Chamar families are on the verge of starvation, Comrade Bishan Das does not give them foodgrains or cash as he desires contradictions to be sharpened and exploded. Similarly, on the religious front, the church priest also does not help them by giving something in cash or kind because he is more interested in their conversion from Hinduism to Christianity. However, the Chamar community did not agree to the suggestion for conversion. Finally, on interpersonal front, a gentleman of matured understanding like Lallu Pahalwan also does not help Kali because men of his caste (Jats) would get annoyed with him. Further, it is true that in the village life there is also village kinship under which girls and boys of even the same caste in the village cannot marry each other as they are treated as brothers and sisters. This social fact prevailing in North India restricts Kali and Gyano to marry. Then Kali goes to church priest and wants to adopt Christianity in case his marriage is allowed but the priest refuses to solemnise their marriage because the girl is simply a minor. Next alternative before Kali and Gyano was to leave the village. But Kali is mentally not prepared to do so, hence when Gyano becomes pregnant, her mother and brother give her poison in order to avoid insult in the community. This depiction of the fear of the community and society in rural Indian context is very realistic.

The message of the novel is that village customs and traditions are deep-rooted and it is very difficult to challenge them suddenly and live in the village at the same time. On the other hand, the poverty of Chamars, due to not holding any piece of land as well as having no alternative occupation, makes them vulnerable and subordinate to the landholding Jats of the village in more than one respect. Therefore, an urgent need, to solve the problem, is land reforms and it is seriously conveyed through this novel from beginning to the end.

In next chapter we will discuss the emerging perspective.

Notes and References

1. V. Shukla (2001), 'Ugra Ka Sahityik Sangharsh', *Vartaman Sahitya*, Issue No. 12, December, p. 8.
2. B. Pandey (2001), 'P.B.S. Ugra Evam Nirala', *Vartaman Sahitya*, Issue No. 12, December, p. 18.
3. Cited in Bharat Bhushan Agrawal (1971), *Hindi Upanyas Par Pashchatya Prabhav*, R.C. Jain Evam Santati, Delhi, p. 95.
4. Nalin V. Sharma (1968), *Hindi Upanyas: Visheshtah Premchand*, Gyanpeeth, Patna, p. 110.
5. Giriraj Kishor (1984), *Parishishta*, Raj Kamal Prakashan, New Delhi, p. 26.

7

The Emerging Perspective

A brief discussion of the scope and subject matter of the discipline of sociology of literature, a relatively new branch of sociology, has been done in the beginning of this study. For the emergence and growth of novel as a genre of literature in Europe, several social conditions such as rise of middle class, increase in education, leisure, printing technology, market, freedom of expression, etc., have been crucial. Afterwards the rise of Hindi novel has been dealt with. Before the Premchand era (before 1918), there were two parallel styles of writing Hindi novels – one being Sanskritised Hindi and the other drawing upon the dialects of common use. Secondly, no conflict of moral values was depicted since most of the characters were presented as following some known values. Thirdly, most of these novels were simple in their structure with focus on some stereotyped story. Consequently, such novels were less realistic. During Premchand era (1918–36), contents of most of the novels were complex. Two schools of novel-writing emerged at that time – one led by Premchand was based on 'humanistic critical realism' while the other led by Pandey Bechan Sharma 'Ugra' and Jaishankar Prasad was based on 'subaltern realism'. Further, there were some women novelists in this era and they concentrated mostly on women-related problems such as those of widows, husband-wife conflicts and prostitution. In the novels of post-independence period, individualism and the increasing gap between the middle and lower classes are major issues. Communalism also attracted the attention of the novelists of this era. In the contemporary period (1981–2010) the diversity of social life has been accorded due recognition. Further, urban centres of varied sizes have been used as bases for writing novels. Women's discourse and dalit discourse have got substantive space during this period. The activities and machinations involved in politics have also attracted the attention of some novelists of this period. Besides, individual fear, disappointment and alienation are also depicted in a number of novels of this period.

Then, dalits and dalit literature have been discussed. The term 'dalit' has been used to refer to ex-untouchables. Over the years dalits have asserted for self-recognition. There are two trends amongst dalit writers: one is to consider dalits *within* the fold of Hinduism and the other is to treat dalits *outside* Hinduism. While the first stream wants change within the Hindu social order, the second one wants to replace it totally. Further, there are three groups of Hindi writers contributing to Dalit literature. The first group comprising of militant dalits is of the view that only a 'born dalit' (ex-untouchable) can write realistic dalit literature because his/her self-experience is authentic. Second group of writers, especially from Other Backward Classes, is of the view that there should be a broad organisational front of dalit and backward class writers to challenge the hegemony of the upper caste Hindu writings. Third group of famous Hindi writers does not accept the exclusive category of 'dalit writers' or 'dalit literature'. They are of the view that for creative writing direct self-experience is not necessary. Writer's world-vision is to be capable of grasping the real situation and expressing it in his creative writings authentically and empathetically. We share the third view.

In the second chapter, 'Theories of Sociology of Literature: A Critique', five major perspectives – realism, socialist realism, Marxist theory, critical realism and postmodernism – have been discussed. Theory of realism explains the causes of appearance of particular writer or his literary creation at a particular time. Thus, it considers literature as an 'external' fact which can be scientifically analysed. It simplifies the relationship between literature and society by neglecting the existing mediations between them. Socialist realism, on the other hand, emphasises on the economic base of a society and class character of the novelist. By applying Marxism mechanically, it searches for 'sociological equivalents' within literary works which are considered as reflections of popularity, ideological position, party affiliation and typicality. Thus, this theory also neglects the mediations between literature and society.

Marxist theory gives importance to the dialectical relationship between author and social conditions and contends that a man is guided by history as much as he makes it. Marx contended that there is no mechanical relationship between artistic creation and economic structure. He terms the writers expressing a class interest directly as mediocre artists and is of the view that only when a writer transcends his own class viewpoints, he reflects truthfully the nature of society and man's relation with it. According to Marxist sociologist, Raymond Williams, a literary activity is a part of culture and there are three kinds of relationship between art and society exist: (a) emphasis on *social conditions* of art; (b) emphasis on *social material* in art works; and (c) emphasis on *social relationship* in art works. One may agree with his last category (social relationship) where there is focus on the 'mediation' or indirectness of relation between experience and its composition, rather than reflection.

Theory of critical realism was propounded by the Frankfurt School of Sociology by synthesising Marxist and Freudian elements. According to this theory, in a modern society of mass culture and art, culture is reduced to an industry and, therefore, alienation destroys the autonomy of culture, art and individual's critical consciousness. It also holds that art, unlike mind, does not have a direct contact with the reality, rather it is set apart from reality. Further commercialisation of art (music, advertisement and cinema) results into the cheapening of art. This aspect is to be noted for sociological analysis of literature in general and of novel in particular.

Theory of postmodernism rejects the empirical view that language can represent reality, rather it is of the view that 'language constitutes' reality. Secondly, meaning is considered local, social, contingent and self-sufficient, and there are meanings and interpretations. Thirdly, here knowledge counts only within a power structure. Fourthly, it questions the 'universalistic' grand narratives like Marxism and liberalism. Fourthly, it gives more importance to difference, decentering diversity and the present (rather than uniformity and history). Finally, it deconstructs texts but forgets to reconstruct it. To our understanding postmodernism is useful in some ways, especially when it links knowledge with power as like religion, polity and economy, knowledge too has power structure. Further, its focus on difference, diversity and decentering is quite useful in analysing literature. But postmodernists should admit that history is as important as important as present, context is as significant as text (no text without context), and reconstruction is as much necessary as deconstruction, it not more. We tend to agree with Rene Descarte's observation: "Divide each difficulty into as many parts as is feasible and necessary to resolve it." Thus, it implies that the deconstruction may be done for the reconstruction, in the ultimate analysis.

After discussing these theories, it becomes clear that the relationship between literature and society is indirect, multidimensional, complex and associational because there are several ways of mediations such as those of author's socialisation, occupational experience, participation in a movement, interaction with readers and other writers, demands of market, electronic printing/technology etc. Hence, a text is to be seen in a context. Secondly, the 'tragic vision' of the author is significant for analysis of a literary work. Three levels of social reality in the Hindi world – political, economic and social – have been analysed as these compete each other at any period. Further, for writing about dalits, one need not be a dalit, rather he should empathise with dalits in order to understand his or her sufferings. None of the four novelists, whose novels have been analysed here, was a born dalit, yet all of them have succeeded in realistically depicting dalit characters and their problems in daily life in proper perspective. Finally, the relationship between form and content of novels is dialogical, dialectical and dynamic.

In the next chapter, 'The Structure of Hindi Novels', an analysis has been done in terms of time and place, characters, events, and inner connections. *Rangbhumi* was published in 1925 when India was under the British rule and masses had launched the freedom struggle under the leadership of Mahatma Gandhi. The story begins in a village Pandepur in Banaras (Varanasi) in UP but it extends later to Rajputana (Rajasthan), Punjab, Garhwal and Poona (Pune) through volunteers for national service. It has sixty-three characters and Surdas (a blind and illiterate dalit) is the central character. Its events are mainly concerned with the colonial regime's anti-people industrialisation policy resulting in the displacement of the villagers. The struggle launched is against the system, on the one hand, and, socio-cultural orthodoxy, on the other. As far as inner connections in *Rangbhumi* are concerned, it may be safely concluded that it indirectly presents a scenario of national freedom struggle and Surdas, through his qualities of non-violence, truthfulness, positive attitude towards women's emancipation and justice represents Gandhi's ideal. Here, Hindu social order is not challenged directly, rather an attempt is made to include dalits within Hindu social order, on the one hand, and forge unity between Hindus, Muslims and Christians, on the other.

Second novel, *Budhua ki Beti,* was published in 1928 when India remained under the British rule. Its story is located in the city of Banaras (UP). There are thirty-eight characters in this novel and Budhua (a dalit) and Aghori (a Brahman) are the central characters. Events of the novel move around the social problems of sweepers, such as, payment of less wages, lack of housing, untouchability, no entry into the temple, lack of education and occupational skills and sexual exploitation of dalit women. As far as inner connections in this novel are concerned, the hierarchical Hindu social order is directly challenged here in order to make it horizontal. Aghori, another central character, is depicted here deliberately because he is a practitioner of the

Tantra cult of Lokayata school of Indian Philosophy with a long tradition of opposing *jati/varna,* and valuing only individual's merits and virtues.

Third novel, *Dharti Dhan Na Apna,* was published in 1972. Its story is based in a Punjab village. There are fifty-one characters in this novel and Kali, a dalit, is the central character. Two parallel stories of socio-economic exploitation for *Chamars* by *Jats* (middle caste), and love affair of Kali and Gyano (both dalits) run through several events. As far as inner connections in this novel are concerned, traditional customs and exploitative pattern of landholdings (dalits being landless labourers) together compound the miseries of dalits. Further, church priest reaches out for conversion of dalits but he refuses to do so for solemnising Kali's marriage with Gyano, especially when she is pregnant and there is a fear of ex-communication by their community. Similarly, communist party leaders do not help the struggling dalits; they do not participate in their struggle nor do they give them doles in cash or kind when dalits are on the verge of starvation. Rather, they take a theoretical stand that the situation is not ripe for the movement and providing doles would amount to compromise.

Fourth novel, *Parishishta,* was published in 1984. Its location extends from a village to a town in western UP and then to Delhi. There are forty-six characters in this novel and Anukul Ram is the central character. The novel moves around events manifesting traditional (caste) prejudices of upper caste students against dalit students even in a modern educational institution. English is valued most. As far as inner connections in this novel are concerned, the novelist tries to forge a broad unity between dalits and the backwards in order to challenge the dominance of the upper castes, though at times the backwards are also shown to discriminate against dalits, (e.g., MP Chaudhuri's wife's discriminatory behaviour towards Anukul and his father). Secondly, amongst dalits themselves, there is intra-dalit community prejudice (between *Chamar* and *Balmiki)* as Anukul's mother expresses her strong reservation at his staying in the hostel with a

Balmiki boy. Finally, there exists some sort of cultural hegemony of English language over Indian language (Hindi).

In the next chapter, 'A Sociological Analysis of Selected Novels', a sociological analysis of the above-mentioned four novels in terms of socio-cultural base, interaction, protest, novelist's background and vision, and a type of realism and message has been made. The socio-cultural base of *Rangbhumi* is rural area extending to the city of Banaras and then to different parts of India. Different castes (upper, middle and lower) and religions (Hinduism, Islam, Christianity) are depicted. As far as interaction is concerned, there are both intra-dalit and dalit with non-dalit interactions. Here caste divisions exist but without caste conflict – though Surdas belongs to a dalit community, he does not face caste prejudices of others, rather he is respected by one and all for his positive qualities.

As far as protest is concerned, Surdas and other villagers protest against colonial regime's policy of land acquisition by force for industrialisation. Secondly, Surdas and Subhagi protest against the attempt of two youths for outraging the latter's modesty. Surdas protests against the fine imposed by Honorary Magistrate making him guilty of adultery with Subhagi. But all these cases of victimisation are not done simply because they are dalits. As far as Premchand's background is concerned, he was born in a lower middle class family of Kayastha (upper) caste in a village in Banaras. He did BA and worked as a teacher as well as a Deputy Inspector of Schools. Being impressed by Gandhi's patriotic speech at Gorakhpur, he resigned from government service in 1921. He successfully transcends his social, cultural and economic background and makes a blind and illiterate man from lower caste and class as the central character of the novel so that the common people get an inspiration to participate in the freedom struggle. Further, he takes the side of suffering women like Subhagi. Finally, his vision exposes the nexus between capitalist class, zamindar class and colonial power. He also presents the cases of transcendence of class – Sophia moves from the capitalist class and Vinay from the *zamindar* class they declass themselves.

As far as the type of realism in *Rangbhumi* is concerned, it is 'humanistic critical realism'. Premchand opposes superstitions, communal prejudices and caste biases. One also finds a broad representation of Indian social reality in his novel since it contains a large number of characters from different backgrounds living together in harmonic and disharmonic conditions.

The socio-cultural base of *Budhua ki Beti* is the urban society of Banaras in UP. Different castes, races, religions and classes have interactions in this novel. In the beginning Budhua makes an individual protest by not cleaning the latrines of any doctor (because his wife died due to discrimination by doctors and poverty) and, later, by the inspiration of Aghori, he organises a collective protest movement which ultimately succeeds due to massive participation of dalits. Novelist 'Ugra' was born in a lower-middle class Brahman family in rural Mirzapur in UP. He was moderately educated. He participated in political and literary movements against the British regime. He transcended his caste and class background and realistically depicted the plight of the sweepers in his novel and allowed their entry into temple as early as 1928 even before B.R. Ambedkar demanded it in 1930s. The message of the novel is that for dalits' liberation Lokayata ideology is appropriate. Further, it also emerges that dalits had no internal leadership from their community in the beginning, hence they require a catalyst agent from outside to inspire and motivate them to launch a movement. This novel's realism is 'subaltern realism', as vividly depicted in the full-fledged movement of scavengers against upper-caste Hindus.

The socio-cultural base of *Dharti Dhan Na Apna* is a village in Punjab wherein upper castes, middle castes and lower castes reside. There are characters from three major religions – Hinduism, Christianity and Sikhism. There are both intra-class and inter-caste conflicts, especially between Jats and Chamars. There are both social and economic protests. The novelist was born in a middle class and caste family in a village in Punjab. He was a student of Economics.

He successfully transcends his caste and class. However, his vision is limited to a protest only, not to a full-fledged movement. The type of realism acted is close to Indianised Marxist realism, but not of orthodox and mechanical type. Rather, it is rooted in Indian soil where there exists both economic and social exploitation of dalits. We get a message from the novel that dalits suffer not only because of caste prejudice (social) and lack of land ownership (economic) but also due to being neglected by the progressive communist party and the religion (Christianity and Sikhism) that does not recognise caste.

The socio-cultural base of *Parishishta* is a village in western UP which extends to an urban centre in western UP and then to Delhi. There are characters from upper castes, middle castes and lower castes in the novel. There is dalit and non-dalit interaction. While some non-dalits such as Khanna, Director and Dean take anti-dalit stand, Neelamma, a non-dalit, supports dalits whole-heartedly. And for this, her image is tarnished by the authorities and students of the IIT, on the one hand, and, on the other, suspicion arises in the minds of the families of Ram Ujagir and Anukul Ram (whose side Neelamma takes). This indicates that while Neelamma stands for class consciousness transcending her caste (Brahman) background, Anukul's father and Ram Ujagir's family do not share that consciousness because of strong caste prejudices in reverse and male chauvinism due to patriarchy. Further, another non-dalit character, Professor Malkani, also supports Ram Ujagir against all odds. There dalit students protest against upper caste students' taunting and discriminatory gestures. Secondly, Ram Ujagir's exploitation leading to his death is also protested by dalit students, Neelamma and Prof. Malkani jointly, indicating the need of some sort broad of unity between dalits and enlightened non-dalits. The novelist was born in a middle class and caste family (of trader) in Muzaffarnagar (UP). He is highly educated. He successfully transcends his middle caste and class background and empathises with dalits in order to present real depiction of their sufferings. His deeper vision of social (caste), economic (costly way of living and maintenance in technical institution) and cultural (dominance of English over Hindi) subordination of dalits makes this novel realistic. He has shown different shades of realism in terms of intra-dalit discrimination (Chamar-Balmiki), middle caste's discrimination (by MP Chaudhuri's wife) and upper caste's discrimination (by students such as Khanna and the higher authorities). This realism is multidimensional cultural realism rooted in Indian tradition where caste also matters along with class and language. Here, one may agree with Prof. Yogendra Singh when he differentiates between occidental and oriental traditions and finally talks of 'modernisation of Indian tradition', that is, modernisation, not westernisation, on the one hand, and Indianness, on the other, should complement each other in a creative way.

The message of *Parishishta* is that there should be class viewpoint cutting across caste prejudices. Secondly, the cultural hegemony of the English language should be overthrown in order to give Hindi its due place. Thus, a novelist should not forget to give a message but not loudly.

After discussing the above, following points of conclusion emerge here:

(a) All four novels are social documentary novels wherein various aspects of the individual and collective life, as it is lived, are realistically depicted. Social reality is multidimensional and complex and therefore its simplification leads to sub-standard literature.

(b) Dalit characters, more often than not, belong to a peripheral group in society, but given due place as central charactess in these novels. However, class matters more than caste in the depiction of social reality and it is necessary for authors to declass and decast for correct and broader understanding of the subconscious, the unconscious and the conscious aspects of dalits' everyday life.

(c) Dalits face both inter-group and intra-group conflicts in their daily life, and conflicts lead to social change by questioning the existing social order or its part.

(d) Dalits protest generally on their own (*Rangbhumi, Parishishta, Dharti Dhan Na Apna*) and also when guided by some catalyst agent (*Budhua ki Beti*). In all these novels, dalits react to and challenge the existing social, political and economic structures in varying degrees. Dalits' 'manufactured consent' (Chomskey) is obtained but they are dissenting openly too.

(e) To realistically depict dalit characters in a novel, it does not seem to be necessary for the writer to be a born dalit. Rather, his world-vision and the capability to empathise with dalits by transcending his social (caste) and economic (class) background can prove to be sufficient for enabling him in carrying out his mission. These four novelists have substantially succeeded in this regard. There could be three ways to capture dalit life: 'swanubhuti' (self-experience), 'sahanubhuti' (sympathy) and 'paranubhuti' (empathy). An author often empathises (keeping oneself in other's place) to understand various arenas of life (from homosexuality to prostitution, from animal world to environment, from beggar to unemployed, from moral turpitude to corruption etc.). Self-experience is neither necessary nor sufficient. Of course, mere sympathy leads to superficiality and mediocrity.

(f) Every novel has a message of some kind – social, economic, political or cultural – connected with a particular time and place. A novel explores new things, it invents reality and therefore a sociologist has to grasp the nuances of newness, invention etc.

(g) The relationship between literature and society is indirect, associational, multidimensional and complex, i.e., there are several mediations between the two and these cannot be ignored while sociologically analysing a literature.

(h) Political, cultural, social and economic levels of reality are competing with one another in India, therefore, it is often difficult for any novelist to decide as to which level is dominant.

(i) For sociological analysis of any literary creation, sociality and literariness are equally significant; hence, one aspect should not be overemphasised at the cost of the other. However, it is emphasised that art for art sake leads from darkness to darkness while art for the sake of life leads from darkness to light ('Tamso ma jyotirgamay').

(j) Since man is a social being, some sort of social relationship exists between man and society – in different forms like 'man in society, 'society in man', or interpersonal relations. Hence, a text is to be analysed in a specific, context (time and place), i.e., sociological imagination (C. Wright Mills) occurs when 'private troubles' change into 'public issues'. Therefore, a sociologist should focus on this dimension in a dynamic-creative and dialectical-critical way while analysing a literary work.

(k) Literature is actually a cultural action for freedom and therefore it may be safely said that literature unites in the ultimate analysis. Literature is not totally a reflection of society, rather it questions status quo and power relations and by raising appropriate questions it indirectly hints at the possible solutions in a latent way. Thus being progressive in nature literature demands cultural diversity just like bio-diversity.

Thus, we are of the firm view that sociological analysis of literature is quite useful in understanding what is manifestly stated, what is latently hinted and what is left unstated and unhinted in a literary creation. Of course, literature is much more than the language (a medium of expression/communication and meaning, a system of signs) and therefore its text may be understood in a better way by locating its context – and there comes 'sociological imagination' (by incorporating biography, history and society), as C. Wright Mills rightly observes.

Bibliography

Abrams, M.H. (1993), *Glossary of Literary Terms*, Prism Books Pvt. Ltd., Bangalore.

Agrawal, Bharat Bhushan (1971), *Hindi Upanyas Par Paschatya Prabhav*, R.C. Jain Evam Santati, Delhi.

Allen, Walter (1954), *The English Novel*, Phoenix House Ltd., London.

Amar Ujala, Meerut, dated 26 February 1996.

Barthes, R. (1977), *Image, Music, Text*, Hill and Wang, New York.

Baudrillard, J. (1975), *The Mirror of Production*, Telos Press, St. Louis.

Baudrillard, J. (1988), *Selected Writings*, Mark Poster (ed.), Stanford University Press, Stanford.

Beach, J.W. (1965), *The Twentieth Century Novel*, Lyall Book Depot, Chandigarh.

Bertens, Hans (1995), *The Idea of the Postmodern*, Routledge, London.

Best, S. and D. Kellner (1991), *Postmodern Theory: Critical Interrogations*, Macmillan, London.

Bharati, Kanwal (1997), *Dr Ambedkar: Ek Punarmulyankan*, Bodhisatva Prakashan, Rampur (UP).

Bharti, C.B. (1996), 'Dalit Sahitya Ka Saundarya Shastra', *Yuddharat Aam Admi*, No. 34–35, April–September.

Brecht, Bertolt (1977), 'Against Georg Lukacs', in Ronald Taylor (ed.), *Aesthetics and Politics*, NLV, London.

Chandra, Jagdish (1996), *Dharti Dhan Na Apna*, Raj Kamal Prakashan Pvt. Ltd. (Paperback), New Delhi.

Curtis, J.E. and J.W. Petras (1952), 'Introduction', in J.E. Curtis and J.W. Petras (eds.), *Sociology of Knowledge: A Reader*, G. Duckworth and Company Limited, London.

Forster, E.M. (1982), *Upanyas Ke Paksha* (Hindi translation of 'Aspects of Novel'), Rajasthan Hindi Granth Akademi, Jaipur.

Fox, Ralph (1956), *The Novel and the People*, Foreign Language Publishing House, Moscow.

Goldmann, L. (1977), *Cultural Creation in Modern Society*, Basin Blackwell, Oxford.

Gramsci, A. (1996), *Selections from the Prison Notebooks*, Orient Longman Ltd., Hyderabad.

Gurtu, Shachirani (ed.) (1955), *Premchand Aur Gorky*, Raj Kamal Prakashan, Delhi.

Habermas, J. (1981), *The Theory of Communicative Action*, Beacon, Boston.

Humphrey, Robert (1958), *Stream of Consciousness in the Modern Novel*, University of California Press, Berkeley.

Jameson, F. (1983), 'Postmodernism and Consumer Society', in H. Foster (ed.), *The Anti-aesthetic: Essays in Postmodern Culture*, Bay Press, Washington.

Kishor, Giriraj (1984), *Parishishta*, Raj Kamal Prakashan, New Delhi.

Kundera, Milan (1992), *The Art of the Novel*, Rupa & Co., Calcutta.

Leenhardt, J. (1977), 'The Sociology of Literature: Some Stages in its History', in J. Routh and J. Wolff (eds.), *The Sociology of Literature*, Keele University Press, Keele.

Lodge, David (ed.) (1972), *Twentieth Century Literary Criticism*, Longman, London.

Lyotard, Jean-Francois (1984), *The Postmodern Condition: A Report on Knowledge*, University of Minnesota Press, Minneapolis.

Madan, Indranath (1981), *Adhunikata Aur Hindi Upanyas*, Raj Kamal Prakashan, New Delhi.

Mannheim, Karl (1982), 'Sociology of Knowledge', in J.E. Curtis and J.W. Petras (eds.), *Sociology of Knowledge: A Reader*, G. Duckworth and Company Limited, London.

Marcuse, Herbert (1970), *One-Dimensional Man*, Beacon Press, Boston.

Marx, Karl (1971), *A Contribution to the Critique of Political Economy*, Progress Publishers, Moscow.

Mills, C. Wright (1959), *Sociological Imagination*, Penguin, Harmondsworth.

Mishra, Girish (1999), *Balzac: Mirror of Modern Capitalism*, Pragati Publications, Delhi.

Mishra, Shiv Kumar (1981), *Premchand: Virasat Ke Swar*, People's Literacy, Delhi.

New Left Review (1984), 146.

Pandey, B. (2001), 'Pandey Bechan Sharma 'Ugra' Evam Nirala', *Vartaman Sahitya*, Issue No. 12, December.

Pandey, Manager (1989), *Sahitya Ke Samaj Shastra Ki Bhumika*, Haryana Sahitya Akademi, Chandigarh.

Patel, Nityanand (1980), *Premchand Ke Upanyas Sahitya Mein Samskritik Chetna*, Lipi Prakashan, New Delhi.

Premchand, Munshi (1999), *Rangbhumi*, Hans Prakashan, Allahabad.

Pritchett, V.S. (1960), *The Living Novel*, Arrow Books, London.

Rai, Amrit (1962), *Premchand: Kalam Ka Sipahi*, Hans Prakashan, Allahabad.

Rashtriya Sahara, New Delhi, dated 26 November 1992 and 20 February 2000.

Routh, Jane and Janet Wolff (eds.) (1977), 'Introduction', in *The Sociology of Literature: Theoretical Approaches*, University of Keele, Staffordshire.

Roy, Gopal (1968), *Hindi Upanyas Kosh*, Vol. I, Granth Niketan, Patna.

— (2002), *Hindi Upanyas Ka Itihas*, Rajkamal Prakashan, New Delhi.

Said, Edward (1989), 'Representing the Colonised', *Critical Inquiry*, Vol. 15, Winter.

Selden, Raman (1985), *Contemporary Literary Theory*, The Harvester Press, Sussex.

Sharma, K.L. (2001), *Reconceptualising Caste, Class and Tribe*, Rawat Publications, Jaipur.

— (2011), *Culture, Stratification and Development,* Rawat Publications, Jaipur.

Sharma, Nalin V. (1968), *Hindi Upanyas: Visheshtah Premchand*, Gyanpeeth, Patna.

Sharma, Pandey Bechan 'Ugra' (1928), *Budhua Ki Beti*, Bisawin Sadi Pustakalaya, Calcutta.

— (1960), *Apni Khabar*, Raj Kamal Prakashan, Delhi.

Sharma, Ram Vilas (1967), *Premchand Aur Unka Yug*, Raj Kamal Prakashan, Delhi.

Shrivastava, Parmanand (1995), *Upanyas Ka Punarjanma*, Vani Prakashan, New Delhi.

Shukla, V. (2001), 'Ugra Ka Sahityik Sangharsh', *Vartaman Sahitya*, No. 12, December.

Singh, Kunwar Pal (1976), *Hindi Upanyas: Samajik Chetna*, Pandulipi Prakashan, Delhi.

Singh, Yogendra (1986), *Modernisation of Indian Tradition,* Rawat Publications, Jaipur.

Swingewood, Alan (1975), *The Novel and Revolution*, Macmillan Press, London.

Watt, I. (1957), *The Rise of the Novel*, The University of California Press, Berkeley.

West, Paul (1965), *The Modern Novel*, Hutchinson University Library, London.

Williams, Raymond (1975), *The Long Revolution*, Pelican, London.

— (1981), *Culture*, Fontana Paperback, Glasgow.

Yadav, Rajendra (1997), *Upanyas: Swarup Aur Samvedna,* Vani Prakashan, New Delhi.

Index